Pocket Billiards
with Cue Tips

EDWARD D. KNUCHELL

Pocket Billiards with Cue Tips is the product of 35 years of active research by the author, Edward Knuchell, one of the prominent masters of the game. Using his first-hand experience as a guide, he has written a clear, informative handbook for those who really want to learn how to play pocket billiards.

Mr. Knuchell's book is appropriate for anyone with an interest in the sport. He begins with the basic elements of the game and builds on these until he is able to discuss the subtlest points of pocket billiards with the same clarity as the simplest. All the details of the play are fully illustrated in 88 diagrams and 40 photographs.

After giving a brief summary of the sport's history, including Mozart's fondness for pocket billiards, the author outlines the necessary equipment and the essentials of play. He moves from there to explain the various games of pocket billiards. Then he outlines certain techniques and exercises that will benefit any player.

The second half of the book is devoted entirely to exploring specific situations that may arise during a game. Here in the CUE TIPS, a feature that he himself invented, Mr. Knuchell pairs diagrams and short, lucid explanations to describe fully the method of play to the reader. Thus the reader can set up any situation he desires and play it again and again until he has perfected his technique.

It is Mr. Knuchell's desire to help bring pocket billiards out from under the shadow of the unsavory reputation it once unjustly held. In *Pocket Billiards, with Cue Tips,* by showing the game in its subtlest and finest points, he does so admirably.

About the Author

Edward D. Knuchell was born in New York City. His primary interests include billiards, travel, and music. In Chicago at age ten he was given a handful of silver by Jake "The Wizard" Schaefer for playing his musical instrument, the Bandonion, and for his pocket billiard shot-making.

At 16 he played and paid his way (with the Bandonion, not the cue stick) to Basle, Switzerland. Later he found himself in the Philippine Islands, where he worked under General John J. Pershing in the Treasury Department. There he married Alice M. Wicks. The Knuchells have one daughter and three sons.

Mr. Knuchell has been awarded two medals; one for playing the Bandonion at age 14 in open competition (the instrument in question is now in the Chicago Historical Society Museum), and the other for playing the piano at the Chicago Musical College. He is now retired in California.

Besides his current book, *Pocket Billiards with Cue Tips,* Mr. Knuchell has written and continues to write numerous articles on the sport. His library on pocket billiards is undoubtedly one of the largest in the world.

Pocket Billiards with Cue Tips

Edward D. Knuchell

Melvin Powers
Wilshire Book Company

12015 Sherman Road, No. Hollywood, CA 91605

Library of Congress Catalogue Card Number: 76-88275

*Diagrams showing shots and position plays by the
author and Bert E. McCormick*

*Posing for stance, cue grip, formation of bridges by
Wayne H. Kendrick*

Drawings by William R. Hampton

Photography by Beem Studios et al

Printed in the United States of America

ISBN 0-87980-069-0

Contents

Acknowledgments

The germ that started this book was latent for 53 years and only through certain unforeseen circumstances did it begin to grow.

First, by the author's retirement;

Secondly, by the encouragement received from many persons including Jake "The Wizard" Schaefer, who praised the author's playing when he was only ten years old.

To the women billiardists of our land.

Introduction

The author's objective:

1. To encourage the women folk to participate in and enjoy the pastime of pocket billiards. The great champion Willie Mosconi said, "The key words in billiard shotmaking are 'soft' and 'softer'." Since a soft gentle touch is so important haven't the women indisputably that particular prerequisite? The fact that more of them are becoming professionals and entering tournaments speaks for itself. The great appeal to women is that pocket billiards is a beautiful and refined game and is ideally suited to them. It is relaxing, beneficial to the health and can be played in the home with husbands, children or friends.

2. To assist the vast numbers of beginners and amateurs who play pocket billiards and who desire to know more about their game. And, hopefully, this book may merit the interest of all billiardists, including the pros.

3. To contribute his little bit toward the advancement of billiards by retrieving the lustre of this old royal game and to do all possible in behalf of the welfare of the professionals to whom so much is owed for the scientific knowledge we have of billiards today. While at lunch with professional Joseph Procita (high run of 182 on a 5 x 10 table, page 100 of *The 1968 BCA Rule Book*) he said there probably were not more than ten out of all the pros who can make a living from billiards alone. What a deplorable situation when you think of how much better off the professionals are in other sports? We are confident

that real progress will soon be made for the well-being of the billiard pros through expanded televised tournaments which will result in more exposure, better incomes and hopefully the creation of benefit and pension funds for them. Among those who are working hard toward attaining these goals there immediately come to mind the names of Brunswick Corporation, Chicago; Billiard Congress of America, Chicago; Billiard Room Proprietors Association of America, New York; and the newly and important Billiard Players Association, Johnston City, Illinois.

1
Historical Notes

A researcher of the Royal British Museum and the author endeavored to obtain all the information possible on the origin and history of the game of billiards. It can be said with confidence that billiards originated in England and France and was taken up as a pastime by royalty and the nobility.

I received a photostat of an excerpt (date, April 7, 1565) taken from her Majesty's State Paper Office, Edinburgh, which reads:

. . . I had the honour to playe a partie at a playe there called the biles[1] agaynste my mestres Beton[2] and I agaynste the Queen[3] and my Lord Darlye,[4] the women to have the gayne of the wynninges. Beton and I havinge the better, my Lord Darlye payde the losse and gave her a ringe and a bruche with two agathes, worthe fyftie crownes. Hereupon depende the a tale that requerethe more tyme than nowe I have to wryte . . .

7 Aprilis 1565. Thomas Randolph[5] to the Erle of Bedford.

"It is a matter of history that Mary, Queen of Scots, when a state prisoner in 1576, complained bitterly of the cruelty of depriving her of her billiard table." This quotation is from *Billiards Through the Centuries* by W. G.

---

1. Billiards.
2. Mary Beaton, Lady-in-Waiting to the queen.
3. Queen Mary of Scots.
4. Lord Darnley who became the second husband of Queen Mary of Scots.
5. Queen Elizabeth's ambassador.

Clifford, printed and published by Printing-Craft, Ltd., 18, Featherstone Buildings, Holborn, London, W. C. 1.

The word billiards stems from the French billard. Apparently the game developed from lawn bowling, which is one of the oldest games played by man. The inclement weather in England was probably the reason why the game was taken indoors and played on the floor. Around the 16th century the game was elevated from the floor to the table—small balls were substituted for bowls, pockets for arches, and the cue for the stick or mace.·

Billiards was introduced in the United States—New York, Virginia, South Carolina, Florida—and was popular during the Revolutionary era. The Library of Congress gave the following information in their letter to me dated August 10, 1967: ". . . most writers place the origin of billiards in northwest Europe of the 14th or 15th century, while some hold that billiards or a similar game was played much earlier in many different places."

The White House curator in his letter to me dated January 10, 1968, wrote: "Our records show that a room on the ground floor of the White House was known as the Billiard Room during the administration of President Chester A. Arthur and through the administration of Theodore Roosevelt. In John Quincy Adams' diaries we find reference to his spending evenings at the 'billiard-table.' " Washington, Jefferson, Lincoln, Chester A. Arthur, and Teddy Roosevelt (to mention only a few of our presidents) played billiards. Great men and women in all walks of life have found pleasure and relaxation playing this game when away from their work and responsibilities.

Henry Ward Beecher wrote about billiards: "The game is a noble one. It should be encouraged in all safe ways. It must be regarded as one of the most charming games that was ever invented. The mind is kept alert and sharp. The whole game is manly, ingenious, and eminently agreeable. It affords a gentle exercise of most refreshing character."

Mozart

Did you know that the immortal composer Mozart was extremely fond of the game of billiards? Michael Kelly in his reminiscences said "Mozart gave me a cordial invitation to his house . . . he was fond of billiards and had an excellent table in his home. Many and many a game have I played with him, but always came off second best." (Ref.: pp. 122 and 127 of book by Otto Zoff, editor, E. P. Dutton & Co., Inc., New York.) Mozart could hardly have had the means to buy this table. In all probability it was given to him. His common complaint was that people showered him with gifts of all kinds except money, which he needed most. The composer's interest in billiards must have helped him forget the poison arrows of vituperation directed against him by jealous contemporaries and also the poverty that stalked him throughout his short life.

Ignace Paderewski also possessed a billiard table in his home. He claimed that playing the game kept his eyes in keen condition.

Mrs. Jane Stanford. (Courtesy of Ralph Hansen, Archivist, Stanford University.)

Opposite is a photograph taken about 75 years ago of a beautifully carved table in the home of Leland and Jane Stanford. For recreation Leland had his horses—460 of them. Jane had her interests too. This recently discovered photo indicates that one of these was billiards. The left-handed shotmaker is Mrs. Stanford; the child, of course, is Leland, Jr.

Ralph Greenleaf, 1900–1950. *(National Billiard News)*

There is general agreement among billiard people that Greenleaf, photograph page 21, is an immortal of pocket billiards; his precise playing, style and magic put him in a class by himself.

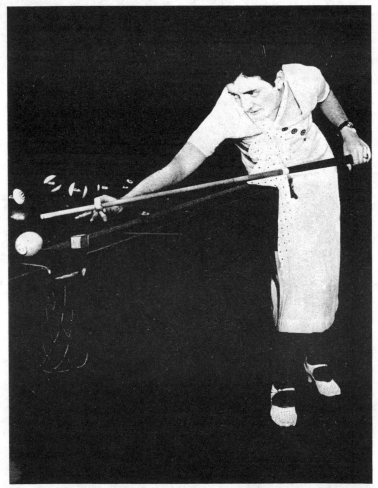

Ruth McGinnis. (*National Billiard News*)

Ruth started playing pocket billiards at the age of ten and became the Women's Billiard Champion of the World and a headliner for 30 years. She represented the Brunswick-Balke-Collender Company for 18 years, giving exhibitions throughout the United States; she also appeared in several Hollywood movies.

For many years billiards bore the status of wealth. Today thousands of Americans of moderate means can and do enjoy this harmless indoor pastime in their homes.

Over 23 million persons play billiards in the United States. More than 100 books on the game of billiards have been published in England; about two dozen in the United States.

2

Pocket Billiards Today

Life rolls on in cycles. Today in the field of sports and recreations it is pocket billiards that is capturing the public's attention and becoming the nation's fastest growing family, home pastime.

Billiard table manufacturers have been making the game attractive to women. The Brunswick Corporation, for instance, was instrumental in doing so when they started planning and outfitting billiard rooms in bowling establishments in California some years ago. These rooms

of ultra-modern design offered the sport to all members
of the family in a setting which billiards had long de-
served. They now have the endorsements of churches,
civic and welfare groups. This company reports that the
response from women who are now enjoying billiards
has been most gratifying and indicative of its appeal to
men, women and children alike.

In consequence there are now many expert pocket
billiard players among the distaff. To mention a few:

Dorothy Wise and Luther Lassiter. *(National Bowlers Journal and Billiard Revue)*

Champions Dorothy Wise and Luther Lassiter pose
with their trophies at banquet, Chicago's Sherman House,
February 1968. Mrs. Wise, an attractive grandmother who
owns and operates Bay Billiards and who is a billiards
instructor in Half Moon Bay, California, believes pocket
billiards is a game perfectly suited for women wanting

relaxation. "You don't need big muscles to compete, but you must have a delicate touch."

Shirley Thayer forms with her husband Cliff the world's finest billiard exhibition team.

Judy Miller entered the Long Beach, California, $21,-000 tournament.

Shirley West's husband is toying with the idea of making his wife into a top-flight woman player. Shirley is not opposed to the idea. West, a professional, started to play various billiard games at age 12 and when he began taking instruction in straight pocket billiards he found the sport challenging and stimulating. "This is really a gentleman's game and an aristocratic sport," he says, "and I think it should be kept that way."

Gail Allums. *(National Bowlers Journal and Billiard Revue)*

Gail Allums, second from right, is a top trophy winner of the 1968 National Intercollegiate Pocket Billiards Championships. The competitors are (l. to r.) Mary Canelos, University of Illinois, third place; Donna Ries, University of Missouri, second; Miss Allums, University of Iowa; and Dorinda Perrin, University of Maine, fourth.

Jean Ann Williams, 21-year-old registered nurse, is the
first woman entry for the women's $500 first prize in the
Billiard Congress of America, U.S. Open Tournament in
Lansing, Michigan.

In Japan where billiards is becoming one of the top
national sports many women are becoming enthusiasts of
the game.

**Noriko Katsura (right), Japan's Women's World's 3-Cushion
Billiard Champion; James Lee (left), billiard mentor; and
Mr. and Mrs. Gordon Bentrod.**

Mrs. Katsura recently gave an exhibition of her skill in Rossmoor Leisure World's billiard room, Walnut Creek, California.

Then there is coming to the public's attention an ever increasing number of child billiardists who are learning and developing skills in their own homes. A few of these who have recently come to my notice are:

This happy crowd pictured at recent U. S. Open Tournament in Lansing, Michigan, moments before they began playing in competition. From left: Evelyn DalDorto, Geraldine Titcomb, Karen Christensen, Jeane Ann Williams, Marion Boyd, Jean Balukas, Sheila Bohm, Chris Miller, Jacquelyn Gorecki, Patricia Greenwald, and San Lynn Merrick. *(National Billiard News)*

Jean Balukas, The Little Princess, 10 years old standing in the middle of the photograph on page 27, started playing at age 3 years. She gives exhibitions and has a fine repertoire of trick shots, which she has performed before numerous television cameras and in elite clubs where even world champions have not set foot. "When I become Champion," she says, "I'm going to take Mommy and Daddy to Florida for a nice long vacation." Jean is the toast of the billiard set in New York.

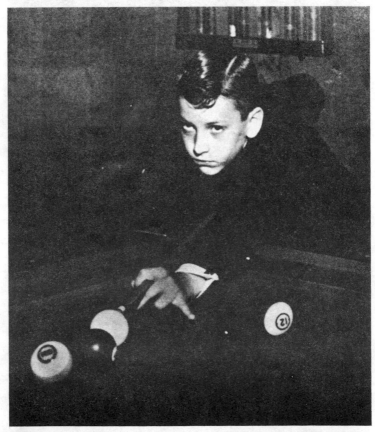

Billy Hosick.

Billy Hosick, opposite, at Napa, California, 11 years old, has made a high run of 47 balls. Although Billy practices many hours a day and has high promise of becoming a great billiardist, he is not neglecting his school studies. He has a good stroke, sharp eye and a hand bridge that is a thing of beauty—classical, professional.

Larry Leake.

Larry Leake, photograph page 29, is from Downey, California. When Larry was in first grade, his Dad thought up a way to help him with his arithmetic. He bought Larry a pocket billiard table and taught him to play and add up his own score. The plan worked and two years later, at age eight, he was not only an A-minus pupil but also one of the most promising billiard artists in the country. The 9-year-old, blond-haired, 4 foot 2, 55 pound youngster has mastered over 25 trick and fancy shots and has already had runs as high as 50 balls in exhibitions. The youngest member of the Brunswick Advisory Staff of Champions, here he "signs" his contract as father, Ray (center), Bob Williams (left), Western Regional Vice President of Brunswick's Bowling & Billiard Division, and Nick Maras (right), Regional Promotion Manager, look on.

3
Learning to Play Correctly

To become a good musician you go to a music teacher. To become a good billiardist you should go to an experienced pocket billiard teacher in your area. If you have difficulty finding one you might write to:

Billiard Players Association, Johnston City, Illinois 62951, or

Billiard Congress of America, 20 N. Wacker Dr., Chicago, Ill. 60606, or

Billiard Room Proprietors Assn. of America, 500 Fifth Ave., N.Y., or

Games Coordinator of the university in your state.

Start right and build a good foundation by learning the proper techniques—stance, cue grip, bridge, stroke and follow-through, striking the cue ball, and hitting the object ball. *And above all, avoid acquiring bad habits.*

It took the author a long time to learn how to draw the cue ball effectively, simply because he did not learn to do it right in the beginning. This illustrates the importance of starting out correctly in order to avoid trouble in the future.

4

Stance, Grip, Bridge, Stroke and Follow-Through

Stance

Your stance should be a natural one, with body comfortable and in good balance; weight equally distributed on both feet. For most shots this means that your body will be turned slightly to the right, feet about six to eight inches apart, left foot forward about 12 inches, with the knee bent just a little. Sometimes it may be more natural for you to shift your weight slightly—to the left foot when you are leaning forward and adding force to

The stance. (Wayne H. Kendrick)

your stroke and to the right foot when you are somewhat farther back from the table and executing soft delicate shots.

When you have to stretch to reach the cue ball, your body will rest against the table and your feet will adjust so that sometimes they may be even with each other.

The grip.

Grip

Beginners are inclined to make the mistake of grasping the cue tightly, often near the end of the handle. Such a grip results in a pump-like motion with the tip of the cue being lowered on the backward stroke and raised on the forward stroke.

Find the balance (fulcrum) point of your cue by balancing it on your finger. Then cradle the handle of the cue delicately in your stroking hand a few inches (not more than six) behind this point. Hold the cue with thumb and any number of fingers (some champions use only one finger, others use two, three and even all four fingers).

After you decide where you want the tip of the cue to strike the cue ball, you must stroke so that you will not miss this important target. For instance, how could you ever develop an effective, snappy, springlike draw shot if you did not hold your cue low and level, and then strike the cue ball at the proper spot below its center? (See Chapter 24 for special technique on the forced draw shot.)

Bridge

The formation of your bridge is very vital because in making a shot, you have to be able to guide the cue accurately from the beginning to the end of the stroke.

There are many variations of forming bridges to execute different kinds of shots. It may come natural for you to favor one over another, according to the size and shape of your hand and fingers. However, learn to use the recommended bridges that have been found to be effective by professionals through experience.

Standard Bridge

This bridge can be used for about 85 percent of all shots. The first thing to do is to spread your bridge hand flat on the billiard table; then raise and bend the index finger, placing the cue under it. Acquire a snug hold of the cue by drawing the thumb, curled index finger and middle finger together. In this position the first joint of your index finger rests against the inside of the first joint of the thumb. Thus, you have the heel of your hand plus thumb and all four fingers giving the bridge comfortable and firm support.

Do not acquire a lackadaisical loose bridge, giving the impression that your fingers do not want to have anything to do with the cue. A loose bridge can allow your

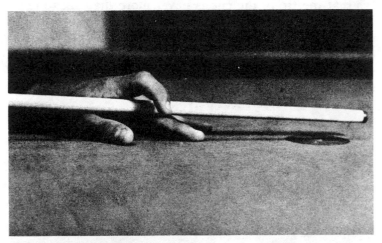

The standard bridge.

cue to shift, and this may spell disaster—missing the shot and losing your inning.

Your bridge should be a snug one, only loose enough

for the cue to slide freely back and forth through it. Also see that the tip of the cue is never more than six to eight inches from your bridge. On draw shots, this distance should be shorter—between four and five inches. On nip draw shots, in which the balls are moved very little, it should be even shorter. In a word, always favor a short distance between bridge and cue tip. This will enable you to stroke more accurately.

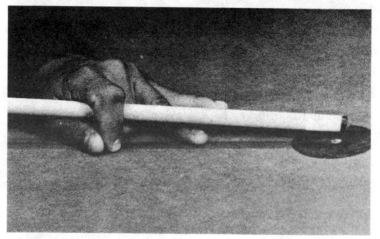

The bridge for draw shots.

Bridge for Draw Shots

The bridge for draw shots is the same as the standard bridge, except that you draw the first two joints of your middle finger under the hand, which helps to lower your whole hand. Shorten the distance between the bridge and the tip of the cue to between four and five inches.

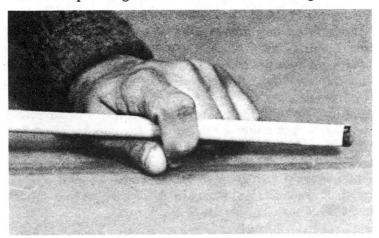

The bridge for nip draw shots.

Bridge for Nip-Draw Shots

For shots where the cue and object balls are very close together, you simply draw in your three fingers and make a fist so that the cue slides only between thumb and curled index finger. Shorten the distance between the bridge and the tip of the cue to between two and four inches.

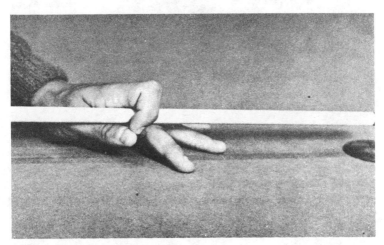

The bridge for follow shots.

Bridge for Follow Shots

For follow shots you use the standard bridge and raise the thumb slightly off the table. In this position, if you have a medium size or small hand with fairly short fingers, you can have the point of your index finger rest against the inside *corner* of your thumb where its nail and flesh meet (as shown in the photograph). You will be surprised to see how professional this bridge then looks. However, remember that your bridge must always be a comfortable and *snug* one. Champion Osaka and former Champion Kubo used this bridge in their San Francisco 1967 tournament. It is classic, looks beautiful, and is one that should meet favor with the ladies.

The bridge for cueing over an object ball.

Bridge for Shooting Over an Object Ball

When striking the cue ball over a nearby object ball, you have to raise your bridge. This is easily done by simply drawing your fingers together, which then automatically raises the whole hand. The three end fingers rest on the table and form a natural tripod. They make a "V" with your thumb through which you can guide the cue.

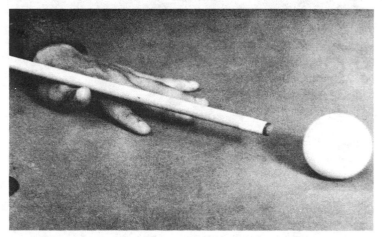

The bridge for shots that require stretching.

Bridge for Shots That Require Stretching

For far-reaching shots you will find it convenient to lay your hand flat on the table and then form a "V" by raising your thumb and the upper knuckles (or middle) of your hand.

Bridge for Rail Shots

When the cue ball is at or near the rail, you can slide the cue over the rail through and under the first and middle fingers. Sometimes you may be able to acquire support by resting your thumb against the outside of the rail; other times by resting your index finger against the inside of the cushion. Then again you may be able to curl your index finger over the cue. According to the position of cue and object balls, the trick is always to adopt a bridge that gives you confidence it is a firm and comfortable one.

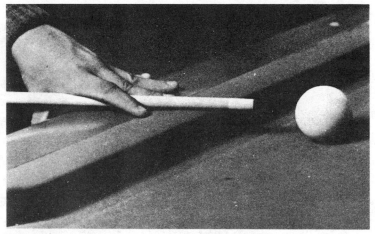

The bridge for rail shots.

Mechanical Bridge

For long shots that you cannot comfortably reach, you should use the mechanical bridge. Lay the bridge flat on the table at an angle to the cue ball, with your left hand resting on it to hold it steady. In stroking, raise elbow and hold the cue between the thumb and first two fingers.

For shooting over a nearby object ball, turn the bridge on end.

In some instances, you will find it preferable to cradle the cue low in the palm of your hand and then stroke with an arm pendulum motion.

In connection with the mechanical or any other unusual bridge,* your stroke should be a smooth follow-through, not jerky, and you must be careful not to commit a foul by touching any of the balls.

*There are really only three basic hand bridges: 1) the standard bridge, 2) the low draw bridge, and 3) the raised bridge for shooting over an object ball.

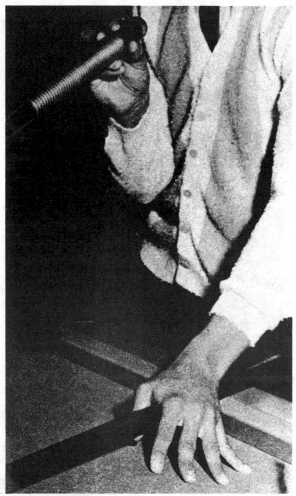

The mechanical bridge.

The mechanical bridge on end.

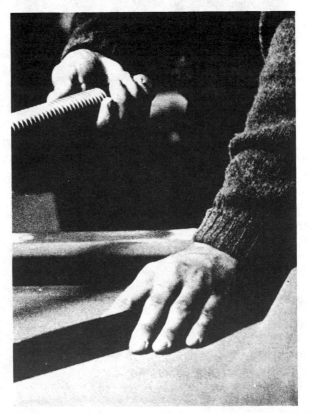

The mechanical bridge cradled in palm of the hand.

Stroke and Follow-Through

Chalk your cue tip before each shot, especially when using English, stretching to reach the cue ball, and using the mechanical bridge. Applying two or three light back-and-forth strokes of chalk will be sufficient. Do not grind (turn) the cue into the cube of chalk.

True Alignment of Eyes, Cue, Cue Ball, and Object Ball
The subject of striking the cue ball (also referred to as cueing or addressing the cue ball) involves several factors:

First of all—to insure accuracy of aim, your head should be directly over the cue with eyes, cue, cue ball, and object ball all in true alignment. In a straight shot to a pocket, this would naturally also include the pocket.

Next, your stroke should be an even, rhythmic one, and one over which you have control of the force applied (known as speed control). That is, you must be able to strike the cue ball with just the sufficient force required to make your shot and obtain good position for the succeeding shot.

The stroke, however, is not complete until you have followed-through with the cue about four inches beyond the point where the cue ball rested before you began the stroke (see Diagram 1). For hard follow shots and hard draw shots you follow-through a little farther.

This very important follow-through action guides the cue and gives additional insurance that the cue ball will correctly contact the object ball so as to drive it in the precise path you intend it to go. If you lift the cue before your stroke is completed, then a slight movement of hands, arms or body may transfer itself to the cue with the result that you may miss your shot.

Of course, it will come naturally for you, as a prelim-

Eyes, cue, cue ball, and object ball in true alignment.

inary just before triggering your shot, to take a few warm-up strokes as a golf or baseball player takes. However, in doing this you must be careful not to touch the cue ball with the tip of your cue; otherwise it may be considered a foul.

Finally, there is the important technique of aiming the tip of the cue to strike the precise spot on the cue ball that each shot calls for; the spot that, in effect, controls that ball.

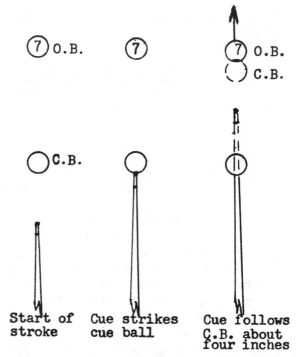

Diagram 1. Sequence of follow-through stroke.

5

The Pocket Billiard Table

For beginners and those not too familiar with a pocket billiard table, reference is made to my new Table Diagram.

The head of the table bears the manufacturer's name. Here you stand when breaking the rack of balls.

Designations have been given to each of the corner pockets and numbers have been assigned to all of the 18 spots (formerly diamonds). I have done this not only to make it simpler to explain at what points of the table to aim, but also to make it easier for you to understand and execute your shots.

The corner pocket designations, spot numbers and rail numbers always remain the same from no matter what side of the table you shoot.

This diagram was submitted to the Rules Authority of the Billiard Congress of America, Chicago, and it has been confirmed that designating the corner pockets and the 18 spots, as I have, is permissible and correct, and has been approved.

* * *

The increasingly popular game of pocket billiards is now in its sixth boom year. Here are some conservative,

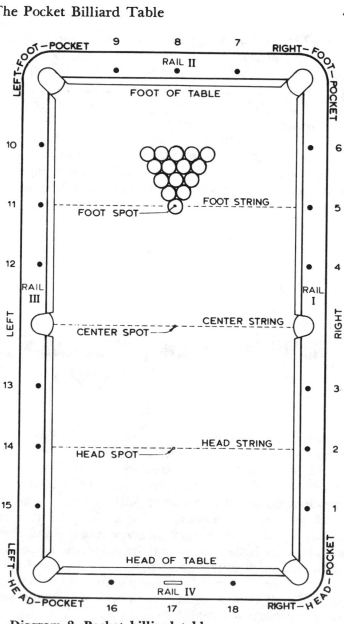

Diagram 2. Pocket billiard table.

educated guesses as to its present status: nonprofessional players, 35,000,000; professional players, 500; commercial tables in use, 125,000; home tables in use, 2,500,000. The commercial table classification includes tables in billiard rooms, lodges, clubs, military posts, and college campuses, but does not include coin-operated tables.

Because pocket billiards is a sport which can be enjoyed in homes as well as at commercial establishments, it is in a solid position for continued growth. It has barely started making a lasting impact on American recreation habits.

6

A Billiard Table in Every Recreation Room

A slogan years ago was "A Chicken in Every Pot." That goal was reached long ago. And now are we on the way to "A Billiard Table in Every Recreation Room"?

Thousands of homes are being remodeled to provide recreation rooms accommodating billiard tables. The reason for this is simply that billiards is an ideal family game and has so many advantages: it gives you leg and abdomen exercise; it can be played by all members of the family; you need only the strength to walk and hold a cue to be able to play it from early youth to extreme old age. And isn't there a saying "members of a family who play together stay together?"

Regarding the care of your own pocket billiard table, every six months you should change the rack from one end of the table to the other. Obviously, this is, to say the least, awkward if your table has gullies at the foot for collecting the balls.

The Heimeshoff family.

Mr. and Mrs. John R. Heimeshoff with daughter Joyce and son Johnny enjoy their home recreation room in Mount Prospect, Illinois. Sometimes they play with their neighbors who also have a pocket billiard table.

Billiard tables are being made better and more attractive all the time. Once so expensive that only the wealthy could afford it, billiards can now be enjoyed by hundreds of thousands of families. Initial investment is moderate; maintenance is very low. Literature you receive from supply houses will explain the various items of equipment that come with the table. However, you may wish to select and make a separate purchase of your own personal two-piece, jointed cue (see Chapter 7).

When colleges and universities put tables in more than 500 student unions, billiards soon became a collegiate competition. More than 12,000 students representing 187 colleges and universities entered preliminary competition leading to the 1968 campus and regional tournaments to determine the 12 finalists. Master Matchmaker Robert Froeschle of the University of Iowa reports: "Recently we've been taking a count of paying customers. We have 300 a day—at least—and more during weekends and nights. We're booked up solid."

There are 743 Boys' Clubs of America (President Richard M. Nixon is Honorary Chairman of the Board) with a total present membership of 730,753. Of this number 80 to 85 percent play billiards. And then at the other end of life, a retirement community is not considered to be complete without one or more billiard rooms. Take, for instance, Rossmoor Leisure World at Walnut Creek, California. Here hundreds of men and women enjoy their two large billiard rooms. Many who have not played for years pick up a cue again. Shown below is a picture of ". . . one of our most enthusiastic players," according to the editor of the Rossmoor News. Until coming to Rossmoor he had not touched a billiard cue for 52 years.

Many claim that walking around and bending over the table is excellent exercise since it is good for the circulatory system. Ladies are taking to the game in ever increasing numbers—this perhaps is because of the beneficial effect on their waist lines.

In San Francisco, Alec Liu has a waiting list for the YWCA class he instructs in his plush country club billiard parlor. He estimates that 40 percent of those play-

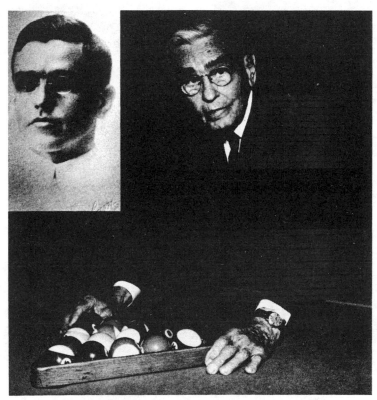

Edward D. Knuchell.

ing in the evening are women, many of them nurses, secretaries, and housewives.

7
How to Buy a Billiard Cue

Ignace Paderewski (1860-1941) always took his Steinway piano with him on his many concert tours in the United States—not as a status symbol (which he did not need) but because he was used to the instrument's "feel," which enabled him to perform with ease and the greatest skill.

Golfers, baseball players, craftsmen, housewives, and others can appreciate Paderewski's desire to use an instrument with which he was familiar in order to achieve excellent results.

Similarly, billiard players have found that they can perform best with the cue of their preference.

When you play with a cue that you are used to, you feel more comfortable. You do not have to make adjustments, and you have more confidence. When you cannot find a satisfactory cue in the cue rack, you have to settle for whatever is available; your playing suffers accordingly.

To start with, you can use the cue which comes with your billiard table purchase. Later on you will, no doubt, want to follow the present trend of selecting and purchasing your own personal two-piece cue with carrying case. However, to avoid costly mistakes, you are advised not to invest in a custom-made cue until you have had enough experience with different kinds of cues. This means months of experimentation and patience in considering such items as weight, length, and thickness of cue, balance, feel, type of handle wrapping, kind and quality of wood, size of tip, and workmanship.

Ladies like a 14 to 16 ounce cue, 54 or 55 inches long, while most men choose a heavier one—up to 20 ounces and 57 inches long.

Proper feel of a cue in your hands is important. Some players like a full feeling cue, while others are more comfortable with a medium or slender shaft. Some like a wide tip; others prefer a small tip. A 12.5 millimeter tip is a favorite size.

A billiard cue is an interesting stick indeed.

Start with the cue's tip, it is made of leather which comes from a water buffalo's or elephant's hide and from the neck of a deer.

The next inch, called the ferrule, is made of buckhorn. The best ferrules are made of special buckhorn that comes from antlers of East Indian deer. The bucks of East India do a lot of fighting, which makes their horns very hard, tough, yet resilient.

The upper, slender, tapered half of the cue is called the shaft. The woods used are mostly maple or ash. The best shafts are kiln-dried rock maple, with the grains perfectly straight and no discoloration or knots or minerals. They should be straight, strong, and springy. The latest, but hardly the best, in cue sticks are those with an aluminum shaft. The chief advantage of these is that they do not warp.

Then, on a custom-made, two-piece cue, comes the joint, made of brass, ivory, or plastic, for coupling the two halves of the cue together.

The lower grip handle is made of birds-eye maple, walnut, Brazilian rosewood, ebony, and other exotic woods. The grip portion is wrapped with leather, Irish linen, or dacron twine.

The last inch or so is made of plastic or ivory for decorative purposes. The owner's name is usually placed here. At the bottom is the rubber bumper for resting the cue on the floor when you are waiting your turn to play.

You can buy an excellent custom made two-piece cue for from $25 to $100. Some players pay even more for them.

8

Various Pocket Billiard Games

All pocket billiard games are played on a rectangular table twice as long as it is wide. The table may be 4' x 8', 4½' x 9', or 5' x 10'. The table generally used is the 4½' x 9', the one used by the pros.

Here is a brief description of each of the seven most popular games:

Rotation

In Rotation the balls are racked as shown in Diagram 3.

The 1-ball is the first object ball until it is legally pocketed. The 2-ball then becomes the legal object ball; then the 3-ball; then the 4-ball, etc.

Rules of the game require that the cue ball must hit

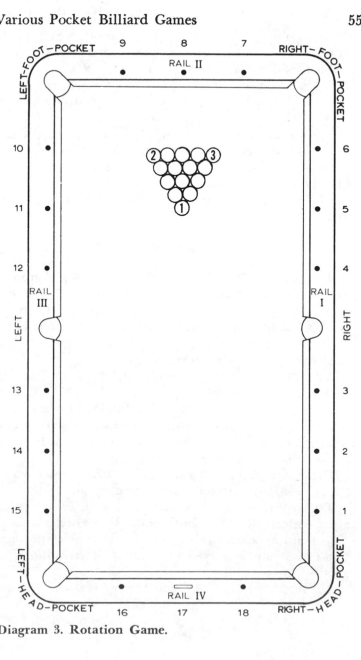

Diagram 3. Rotation Game.

the legal object ball before touching another ball. Failure
to do this is a miss and ends the inning. Balls pocketed
on an illegal contact are spotted.

If a player makes a legal contact on the object ball he
is entitled to all balls pocketed on that stroke, whether
or not he pocketed the legal ball.

The Rotation game is chosen by some players because
they like the element of luck that they think may be on
their side. However, this game can be played very scien-
tifically, so that if your opponent has excellent cue ball
control you may be utterly outclassed and have no chance
to win.

Line Up

The balls in Line Up are racked as in 14.1 Continuous
Pocket Billiards (see Diagram 4). It is a call-shot game,
players being required to call the ball and the pocket.
If a called ball kisses before entering the called pocket,
it counts. Likewise, if a called ball banks several times and
then enters the called pocket, it counts.

All balls scored are spotted on the long string line. The
long string line is an imaginary line from spot 8 to the
foot spot. Some tables show this line with black pencil
to help the players line up the balls straight. Consequently,
before each player takes his turn there should be a total
of 15 balls on the table.

Game is an agreed upon number of points—it can be
25, 50, 100, or whatever score agreed upon.

The requirement for precise playing in Line Up is on
a par with that of 14.1 Continuous. The scoring is simple.
The main appeal of this game is that it is easily understood and can be played in a spirit of friendliness and
good-will.

For suggested Line Up Game safety breaks see Diagrams
7, 8 and 9.

14.1 Continuous (Championship Game)

In 14.1 Continuous the balls are racked as shown in Diagram 4. It is a call-shot game, players being required to call the ball and the pocket.

This game is the one the pros play in their championship tournaments.

Starting player must drive two or more balls to a cushion in addition to the cue ball or cause an object ball to drop in a pocket. (If he drops a ball in a pocket he does not get credit for that ball unless he called the shot.)

After 14 balls have been pocketed they are racked with no ball being put on the foot spot.

The 15th ball, which has been left on the table, is then used as a break shot, that is, the player pockets it from the position where it rests on the table and tries at the same time to have the cue ball break up the newly racked 14 balls. If the 15th ball (that is, the last ball of the 15) rests within the racking area, it must be spotted on the head spot. For other interferences with the racking of balls see *The Official Rule Book*.

For keeping score in this game it is advisable to use a counting string. When starting a new rack of 14 balls, each player leaves a space between his previous total count and the 14 balls of the new rack; this in order to be able to always account for the 14 balls of each new rack.

See Diagram 9 for 14.1 Continuous safety break.

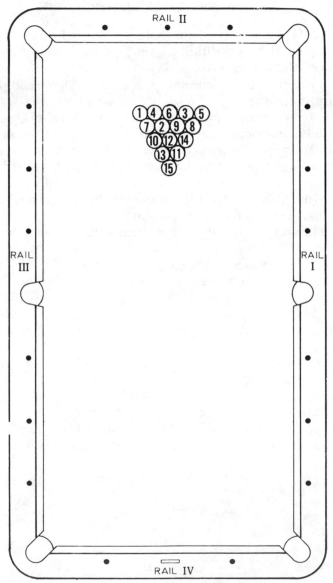

Diagram 4. 14.1 Continuous Game.

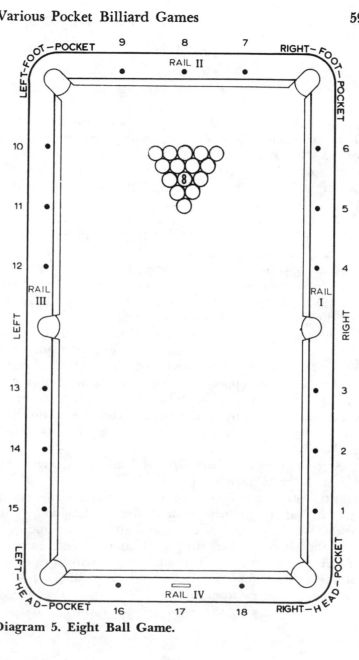

Diagram 5. Eight Ball Game.

Eight Ball

The balls in Eight Ball are racked as shown in Diagram 5.

One player or side must pocket balls numbered from 1 to 7 or from 9 to 15. The opponent pockets the group of balls not selected by player with the original choice. The order of play can be determined by lag or lot. The player or side pocketing a numerical group first and then legally pocketing the 8-ball wins the game.

If the opening player pockets one or more balls on the break, he has his choice of the high or the low group, the latter or opponent's ball would not be spotted. Whenever an opponent's ball is made, it is never spotted. If the breaker fails to pocket a ball on the break, the incoming player accepts balls in position and has his choice of the high or low numbered balls.

The striker is entitled to all balls legally pocketed, unless he pockets a ball belonging to his opponent, in which case, the opponent is credited with that ball. If a player pockets only an opponent's ball and none of his own group, it is a miss. A player must always hit one of his group of object balls first. If this is complied with, then any ball of his group pocketed on the shot is legally pocketed.

According to *The 1968 Official Rule Book,* Eight Ball is lost in the following ways:

If the player shooting directly at the 8-ball fails to cause the cue ball to go to a cushion after hitting the 8-ball, or the 8-ball to contact a cushion, he loses the game.

If the player pockets the 8-ball on the break or if the player pockets the 8-ball accidentally during the course of the game before he pockets all the balls of his numercial groups, he loses the game.

When playing for the 8-ball, player must hit that ball

first. If he pockets the 8-ball on a combination, he loses the game. If he fails to hit the 8-ball on the bank, he loses the game.

Since a player is required to call his shot when playing for the 8-ball, he loses the game if the 8-ball drops into a pocket not designated on the call.

When a player is shooting to make the 8-ball, he loses the game if the cue ball scratches in pocket.

*   *   *

It is simple to keep score in Eight Ball. It is one of the shortest games, and is a great equalizer; that is, an inexperienced player has a chance to win against a superior player.

American Snooker (see Diagram 87 for racking of balls)

The American version of this game (which is a favorite in Canada and England) is played with 21 object balls and a white cue ball on a 5-by-10 or a 6-by-12 foot table. The game is also played on 4-by-8 and 4½-by-9 foot tables. The balls used are only 2⅛ inches in diameter; cues average 60 inches in length and 12 to 19 ounces in weight.

Fifteen of the object balls are red. Each red ball has a scoring value of one. The other six object balls are:

Yellow, with a value of 2.
Green, with a value of 3.
Brown, with a value of 4.
Blue, with a value of 5.
Pink, with a value of 6.
Black, with a value of 7.

The game may be played by individuals or sides. The highest score at the termination of the game determines the winner, the game ending when all the balls are off the table. The winning score is indeterminate, since points and forfeits enter into the final accounting.

Because the rules of the game, including fouls, penalties, forfeitures, etc. are numerous, it is suggested that for a thorough knowledge reference be made to Billiard Congress of America's *Official Rule Book.*

Because the games of Nine Ball and One Pocket are being included in today's tournaments for professionals, I am adding a brief description of these two games:

Nine Ball

Nine Ball is played with a cue ball and nine balls numbered one through nine (see Diagram No. 6). Balls are racked in a diamond on the foot spot with the 1-ball at the apex of the triangle and on the spot, the 2-ball on the left corner, 3-ball on the rear corner, 4-ball on the right corner and the 9-ball in the center of the diamond behind the 1-ball. The object of the game is to legally pocket the 9-ball. This is not a call-shot game, as opposed to 14.1 Continuous and Line Up games.

When the opening shooter hits the number 1-ball, first, the shot is legal and anything pocketed shall be scored for the shooter. From this point the shooter must always hit the lowest numbered ball on the table. If this basic rule is complied with and no fouls occur, then anything pocketed is considered legal. No ball that has been legally pocketed shall be returned to the table as a result of fouls. Penalties shall be loss of turn only.

One Pocket

The game One Pocket is played with a cue ball and 15 numbered balls. No particular order of racking the balls is required. Option to break is determined by lag or lot, and prior to the opening shot, one pocket at the foot of the table is selected by the winner of the lag as the pocket he will use. The other person or side will then use only the other pocket at the foot of the table.

The first player to legally put eight balls in the pocket

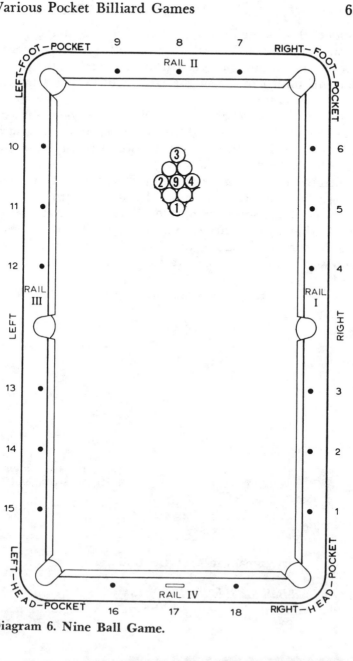

Diagram 6. Nine Ball Game.

assigned him shall be declared the winner of the game. Should a player accidentally put a ball in his opponent's pocket, the opponent gets credit for the ball and the player loses his inning unless in the same shot he put a ball in his own pocket.

In order to play safe on the break shot, only the cue ball or one object ball ought to be driven to a rail whereas in the 14.1 Continuous game two balls plus the cue ball should be driven to a rail.

Before this game gets underway players usually arrange to switch pockets each game for the sake of fairness.

Many of the shots in the One Pocket game are safety shots, whereby one tries to put balls near his pocket leaving the cue ball in such a position as to make it well-nigh impossible for his opponent to put a ball in his own pocket.

For three safety breaks in this game see Diagrams 59, 60, and 61.

9

The Break Shot

Breaks in Line Up Billiards

The Head-Ball-for-Side-Pocket Break
Place the cue ball behind the head string at a point

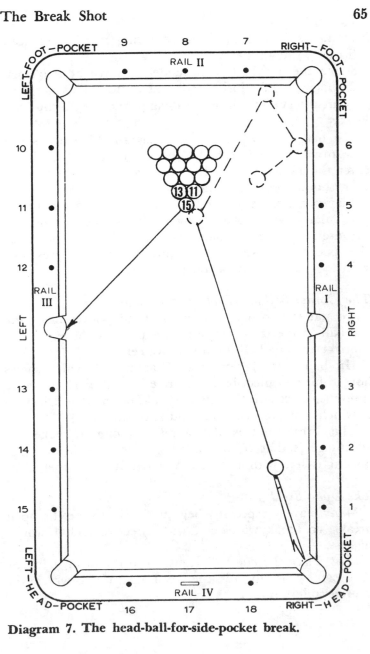

Diagram 7. The head-ball-for-side-pocket break.

four inches from Rail I (when trying to put the head
ball in the side pocket).

Strike the cue ball with moderate force at 9 o'clock
(see Diagram 10), just a trifle off center. This helps to
prevent the cue ball from scratching into the Right-Foot-
Pocket.

Hit ball 15 at ⅔ right (see Diagram 12 which shows
how to hit an object ball) and then watch the 15-ball
enter the Left-Side-Pocket. (See Diagram 7 which, however, shows no burst of the rack.)

Players are sometimes reluctant about using this break,
particularly when playing against a strong competitor,
because it spreads the balls too much. If the shot in the
side pocket is missed, then your opponent is presented
with too many easy shots on the table.

The Corner-Ball-for-Head-Pocket Break

To put the corner ball in the head pocket place the
cue ball in the same position as explained above.

Strike the cue ball a trifle above center.

Hit ball 5 at ⅝ right (see Diagram 12, which shows
how to hit an object ball) to drive it to Rail II and have
it bounce back into the Right-Head-Pocket. (See Diagram
8, which, however, shows no burst of the rack.)

This break shot is also a difficult one to make. Its
advantage is that if the called ball is missed, your opponent is left with but few opportunities on the table.

The Open Break

Many players, especially beginners, like to use the open
break. To break wide-open with effective luck I would
suggest:

First. Place the cue ball right up to the head string or
back somewhat towards the head rail (IV), whichever
is preferable for you.

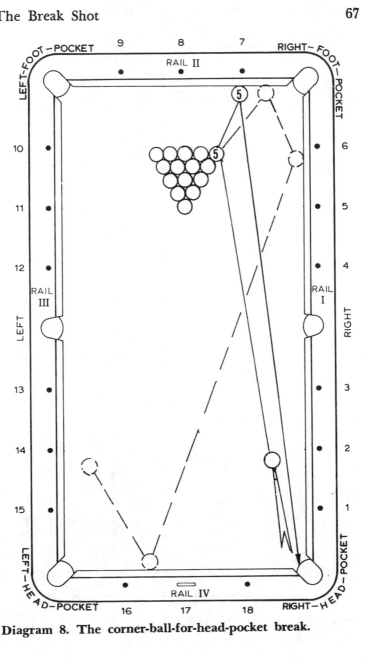

Diagram 8. The corner-ball-for-head-pocket break.

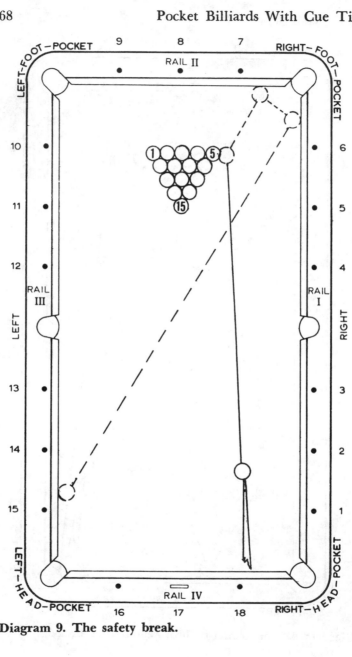

Diagram 9. The safety break.

Second. Stroke hard at dead center throwing the weight of your body forward with the stroke but not with such force that you miscue or lose your aim and hit the head (apex) ball significantly off center.

Safety Breaks

14.1 Continuous Game Safety Break

The 14.1 Continuous Game Safety Break is the one used by professionals and advanced players. It is also sometimes used in the Line Up game. The usual technique is to use right English when breaking on the right side of the table, hitting the 5-ball thinly with a soft stroke so as to drive it to the end rail and back to the rack and drive the other corner ball, the 1-ball, to the left side rail and back to the rack. The cue ball hits two or more cushions and comes to rest near the Left-Head-Pocket where it is farthest away from all the object balls and consequently in a disadvantageous position for your opponent. (See Diagram 9, which, however, shows no burst of the rack.)

One Pocket Game Safety Break

For three safety breaks in the One Pocket game see Diagrams 59, 60, and 61, Part 2 below.

10
How to Improve

When I observe players at a pocket billiard table, I try to figure out just what makes things click for one person and not for another.

I cannot help but think it must be the same ingredients that are present in every other of life's professional endeavors, namely:

A—A person may be endowed with transcendent ability, as a genius is.

B—He is especially equipped mentally and physically to excel in the particular thing at hand.

C—He has limited ability but continues on because he is so interested in what he is doing that hard work, perseverance, and patience become a pleasure rather than a task.

It is understandable how one can move from Group C to Group B, but I think you will agree that Group A is unattainable unless you are born into it.

How then can beginners and the vast majority belonging to Group C hope to improve their playing ability?

First, correctly learn where to have the cue ball hit the contact point of the object ball so as to successfully make the shot.

Second, learn position control—having the cue ball come to rest at an advantageous spot for the succeeding shot. This brings into play the techniques of follow, stop, near-stop, draw, English, and speed control.

Third, learn to practice in a purposeful and concentrated manner. When you miss a shot, replace the cue and object balls and try the play over and over to discover *why* you missed and how you can correct your error and improve your execution of the same shot when it comes up in regular play.

Fourth, think in a positive way. If you think on the negative side, then you will keep fumbling along. For example, if you think you are going to miss, then the chances are you will do just that very thing. The thought of missing must be shaken off; you must readjust yourself, try hard to control your thinking and aim carefully again before triggering the cue ball.

Fifth, in playing the call-shot games of 14.1 Continuous and Line Up make it a part of your routine to examine clusters for "on" shots. These hidden shots save a player from going for a difficult shot and, more importantly, they afford him the opportunity to spread the balls, thus enhancing the chances of continuing his run of balls.

11

Last Glance before Triggering the Cue Ball

The question is often asked: "Do you look at the cue ball or the object ball last, at the very instant that you strike the cue ball?" There is not unanimous agreement on this. The answer given me by a professional pocket billiard player was that you look at the *cue* ball last to be sure you strike it at the correct spot with the tip of the cue.

Well, that may be all right for him or others, but for me, when I was learning and tried that, the object ball did not roll in the precise direction it was supposed to go, and in one instance it came closer to rolling into the Left-Foot-Pocket instead of into the Right-Foot-Pocket. So I could not take his advice.

I like Willie Hoppe's answer to this question because I think he wanted to be fair and honest about it. He said, "My eyes are last on the cue ball." But he quickly added, "Both methods are satisfactory. Anyway, you do this automatically and unconsciously."

However, it must be remembered that while Hoppe was a universally acclaimed great all 'round billiard player, he was greatest in the cushion billiard games. Because so much English has to be used in these cushion games (on perhaps 80 percent of the shots), it is extremely important to be very careful and accurate in striking the *cue ball.*

In pocket billiards, which calls for much less English, hitting the *object ball* correctly becomes of paramount importance. *Practically all pocket billiard professionals advise looking at the object ball last.*

For a long time I made difficult shots and missed easy ones. Suddenly it dawned upon me that when I intended to strike the cue ball right in the center I must have, at the very last fraction of a second, moved the point of the cue tip slightly, so as to put in motion either left or right English, making me miss the shot. I now adhere to the following:

A—Size up the position of the cue ball, object ball, and the pocket.

B—Determine whether to strike the cue ball in the center or to the right or left; then position the tip of the cue firmly at the correct spot, *and hold it there.* These four italicized words are extremely important.

C—Look back and forth from cue ball, to object ball, to pocket. Keep your eyes *on the object ball at the precise last moment* before triggering the cue ball.

It would be ideal if you could look at all three objects simultaneously when you are ready to shoot, but that is not possible.

One time, on a difficult shot, I thought I had accomplished the feat of simultaneously looking at the object ball and pocket when striking the cue ball. I felt positive then that I would make the shot, and I did.

It certainly is not possible for you to look at cue ball, object ball, and pocket all at the same time unless you have a special sense of vision or wear a trick pair of trifocals.

12

Striking the Cue Ball—Clock-Dial Method

The "open sesame" to acquire cue-ball control is knowing the exact spot where the tip of the cue must strike the cue ball and using the correct stroke force.

I recommend the Clock-Dial Method as a simple guide to indicate and help you visualize where this contact should be made when the use of English is called for. There are four basic types of English, namely: 1) top or follow, 2) bottom or draw, 3) right, and 4) left. More about this subject in general in Chapter 14.

Consider the cue ball as having the face of a clock with hours and minutes dividing the 360 degrees. Thus you use the numbers 1 to 12 (standing for the positions of the hours) to impart the specific English:

    12, for follow
    1, right follow
    3, right English
    5, right draw
    6, draw
    7, left draw
    9, left English
    11, left follow

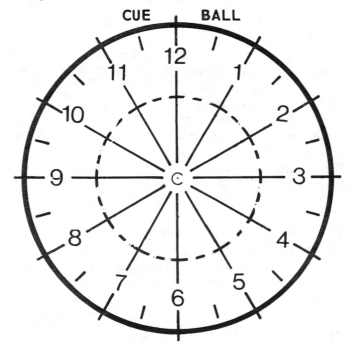

Diagram 10. Cue ball.

In addition to these eight basic strokes, there is the important dead-center stroke.

The purpose of using the nine different kinds of strokes above is to have the cue ball hit the object ball, pocket it, and then come to rest at an advantageous spot for your succeeding shot.

In all these strokes the tip of your cue must contact the cue ball *within* its imaginary *inner* circle that divides the ball in half—either at its dead center for a center shot or at a point away from this spot not more than the width of the tip of your cue.

There is one exception to this rule and that is in the

case of a draw shot. Here, when you want maximum draw action, you may strike the cue ball as low as is reasonably safe without miscueing. And of course to help you from miscueing you must remember to give the cue tip the usual few strokes of chalk.

You impart varying degrees (shades) of English, depending upon just where you stroke the cue ball beyond its dead center. The farther away from center, the more you accentuate the spin of the cue ball.

Professionals sometimes use extreme English beyond this inner circle on shots when it is needed. There is always the danger in striking outside the inner circle that you will miscue.

For all shots your cue should be held level, particularly in executing draw shots. The only exception here would be in executing massé shots requiring near perpendicular elevation of the cue (see photograph of Noriko Katsura, page 26) and for jump shots requiring about 30 percent elevation of the cue handle. For the jump shot see photograph below; also see Diagram 82 in Part 2.

The jump shot.

Unless you are a professional, it is better to not use the jump shot because of the danger of damaging the table felt.

I like the clock dial method—it is easily designated and comprehended by everyone. It is so precise that when I explained it to a friend he began designating where he would strike the cue ball by even using minutes, such as 3:30 o'clock. Actually, "o'clock" is seldom used.

13

How to Pocket a Ball

This chapter brings us to the crux of pocket billiards—sighting the shot.

Contact Point

The contact point is the point at which the cue ball must hit the object ball in order to pocket it. You can definitely establish this point in a number of ways:

First, take the cue itself and make as if to strike the object ball so as to drive it to the center opening of the pocket. Where you thus would strike the object ball with the tip of the cue shows the correct contact point for a full-ball shot; see A in Diagram 11.

Second, lay two object balls (I have used 2 and 3) together so they are in direct alignment with the center

opening of the pocket. The point at which ball 3 touches
ball 2 shows the correct contact point. To prove this re-
move ball 3, then strike and drive the cue ball so that
it will precisely take the position that ball 3 occupied.
This will guarantee your pocketing ball 2. See B in Diagram 11.

Third, draw a line from the center opening of the
pocket to and through an object ball as I have done with
ball 4. The end of this line, where it meets the outer sur-
face edge of the object ball, shows the correct contact
point. See C in Diagram 11.

Diagram 11-C shows two angle shots to a corner pocket.
It shows why in angle shots you must *not* aim at the contact point. The reason for this is simply that in dealing
with spheres the side of the forward curvature of the cue
ball meets the side of the front curvature of the object
ball at a half-way point (the contact point).

CUE TIPS: As you know, all 15 object balls are numbered
and 7 of these are striped. It quite often happens that in
angle shots the contact point is in a location that bears a
definite relation to either the number of the object ball
you decide to pocket or a portion of it, or to the middle
or one side of the object ball's stripe. It consumes only
a second to take note and advantage of this so that when
you move back to your cueing position, you can remember
and visualize where the contact point is.

Point of Aim

Pocket billiards sighting is difficult because there are
only two shots that offer definite targets—the full-ball shot
and the half-ball shot. See Diagram 12.

Full-Ball Shot: In this shot the cue ball, object ball and
center of the pocket are in a straight line. You have only
to be careful that your stroke is what is called for—a

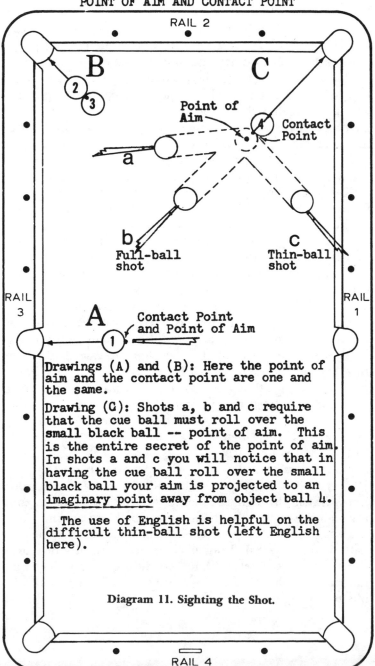

RAIL 2

B

C

Point of
Aim

Contact
Point

a

b
Full-ball
shot

c
Thin-ball
shot

RAIL
3

RAIL
1

A   Contact Point
    and Point of Aim

Drawings (A) and (B): Here the point of
aim and the contact point are one and
the same.

Drawing (C): Shots a, b and c require
that the cue ball must roll over the
small black ball -- point of aim. This
is the entire secret of the point of aim.
In shots a and c you will notice that in
having the cue ball roll over the small
black ball your aim is projected to an
imaginary point away from object ball 4.

The use of English is helpful on the
difficult thin-ball shot (left English
here).

Diagram 11. Sighting the Shot.

RAIL 4

straight one. Aim directly at the contact point of the object ball. *This is the only shot where the contact point and the point of aim* are one and the same.

Half-Ball Shot: In this shot you aim directly at the outer edge of the object ball which makes this a very important and advantageous shot in gauging it and related shots. In all other angle shots the player has to use his best judgment. However, here is good news. Since the object ball is 2 2/8″ in diameter and a corner pocket is 4⅞″ minimum wide and a side pocket is 5⅜″ minimum, there is considerable margin for error in pocketing a ball *when it is near a pocket.* The margin for error diminishes the farther away the object ball is from the pocket and the more accurate you then must be in order to make the shot.

After you have determined all the phases of the angle, start sighting from your hand bridge to the cue tip, through center of the cue ball, thence to the point of aim. This can be done best with a low stance bringing the eye down to the cue as low as is comfortable. When not satisfied with my aim on a long difficult angle shot I check it by first aiming to cut thinner than necessary and then thicker than necessary in order to arrive at a median of the two—the cut that I feel is the correct one. If you have correctly calculated the angle and your stroke is perfectly executed then the cue ball and the object ball will hit each other at the *magic contact point*, which will successfully pocket your ball.

Now let us consider the principles involved. Diagram 12 (1) shows an object ball and a cue ball with four lines drawn through the center of the cue ball to and through the right half of the object ball and another four lines beyond the edge of the object ball. Having the cue ball hit the object ball on its right side naturally produces throw-offs to the left. (The left side of the object ball must receive the same consideration for object ball throw-offs to the right.)

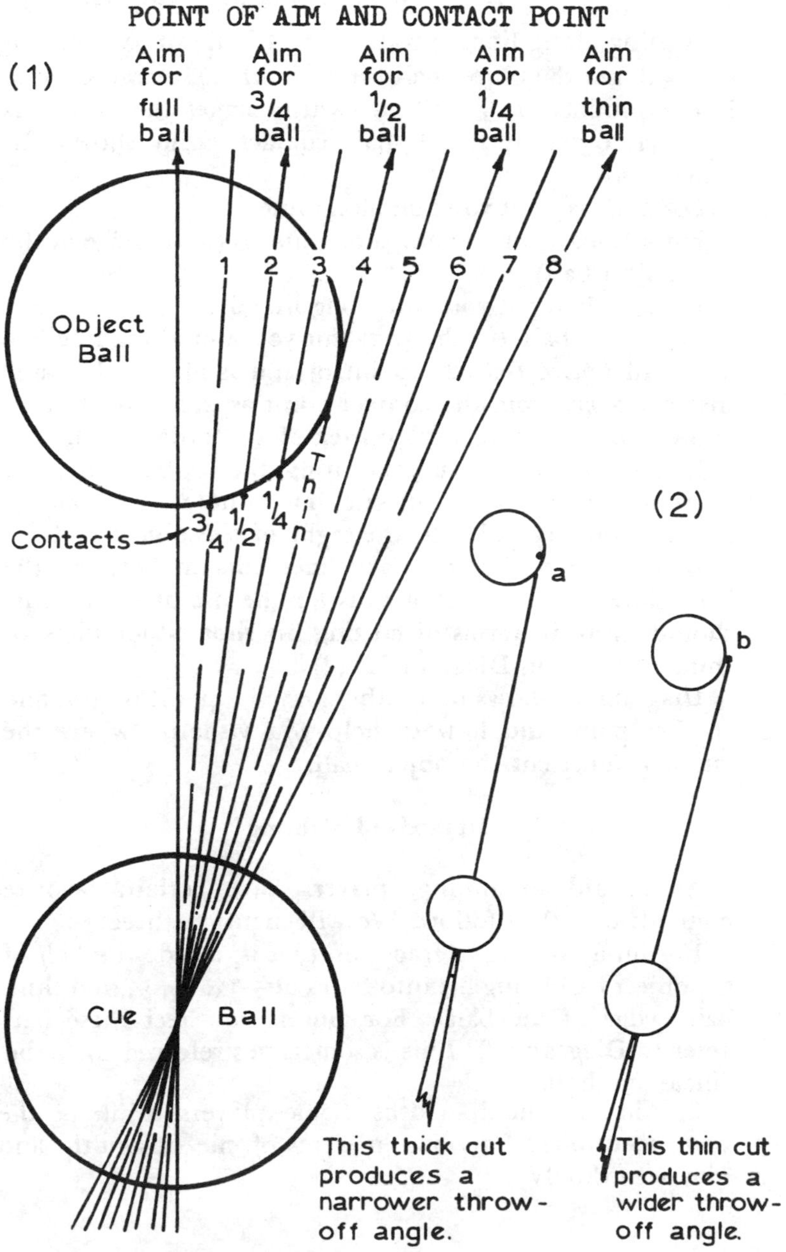

POINT OF AIM AND CONTACT POINT

Diagram 12. Cutting the Object Ball.

Aiming along line 1 produces a ⅛-ball cut (where the cue ball and the object ball hit each other). Aiming along line 2 produces a ¼-ball cut which makes the two balls hit each other at the ¾-ball contact point shown. In other words:

For a ¾-ball cut you aim along line 2

For a ½-ball cut you aim along line 4 (outer edge of the object ball)

For a ¼-ball cut you aim along line 6

For a thin-ball (feathering) cut you aim along line 8

You will notice that the point of aim is always the same distance away from the contact point as the contact point is away from the vertical center of the object ball. You will also notice that in executing the ¼-ball cut shot (line 6) and the thin-ball cut shot (line 8) your aim is at an imaginary point to the right of the object ball.

If a player wishes to make finer cuts in between the lines shown, or if the shot calls for the use of English, he should think in terms of cutting his shot either thick or thin, as shown in Diagram 12 (2).

Diagram 13 shows in another way the point of aim and contact point and how to help you visualize where the cue ball must cut the object ball.

Methods of Sighting

As an aid to aiming, players have certain favorite methods that they follow. We will mention three:

1. Aim according to fractions, that is, divide the *half* of the object ball being hit into four cuts—¾, ½, ¼ and thin-ball (edge of the ball). For aiming to effect these cuts refer to Diagram 12. This is sometimes referred to as the linear method.

2. Aim by cue-tip-widths. Some players think of the abovementioned fractions in terms of cue tip widths and aim accordingly.

POINT OF AIM AND CONTACT POINT

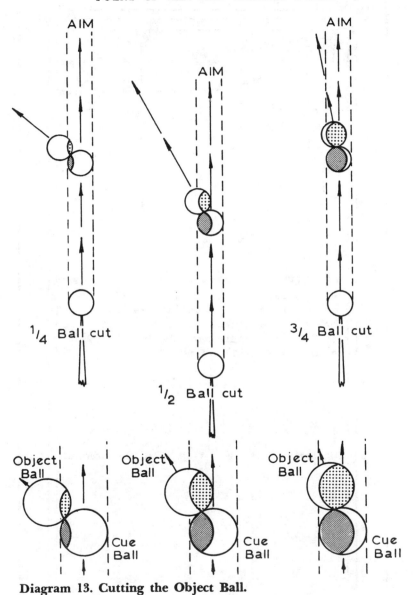

Diagram 13. Cutting the Object Ball.

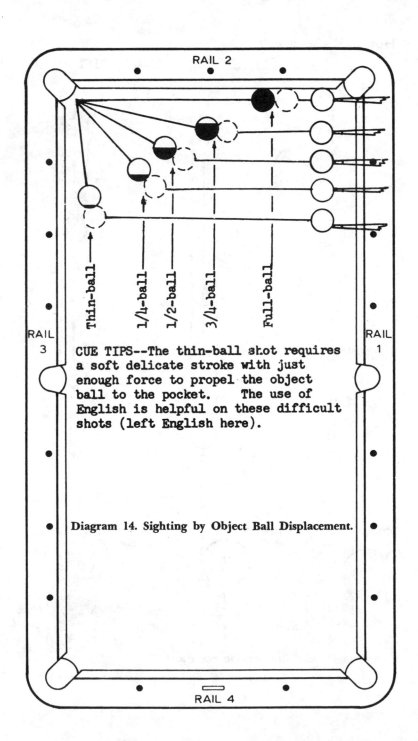

RAIL 2

Thin-ball

1/4-ball

1/2-ball

3/4-ball

Full-ball

RAIL 3

RAIL 1

CUE TIPS--The thin-ball shot requires a soft delicate stroke with just enough force to propel the object ball to the pocket. The use of English is helpful on these difficult shots (left English here).

Diagram 14. Sighting by Object Ball Displacement.

RAIL 4

3. Aim *on an area* by having the cue ball cut out the hidden area of the object ball that the cue ball must replace to effect the correct contact. In other words instead of envisaging an invisible point you think in terms of sighting by object ball displacement. England's world's champion snooker player Joe Davis, who has written seven books on billiards, is a strong advocate of this method, which he explains and illustrates photographically. (This reference to Mr. Davis's method is made by permission of The Hamlyn Publishing Group Limited from *Advance Snooker* by Joe Davis published by Country Life Limited.) See my interpretive Diagram 14.

Four diagrams, numbers 11 to 14, have been presented so that from one or another you may better understand the mechanics, the principles involved. However, when at a billiard table you cannot refer to diagrams; instead of the draftsman's product you are now up against the practical know-how of the thing. Quick calculations must be made and fixed in your mind's eye of the entire shot before you start stroking.

No particular aiming method is urged because I believe each player should follow the method he prefers— the one that fits his personality, mentality or whatever it is that makes things click for *him*. Anyhow, after becoming an advanced player he gradually and naturally drifts away from what he first started with and then relies on the real thing—*experience, instinct* and *feel*.

My billiard library contains over 100 books.*

*In the books explaining the contact point and the point of aim there is general agreement on the former. However, in some books, the point of aim is not well explained and illustrated; in several instances the presentation is faulty. In my opinion Richard Holt in his book *Billiards and Snooker*, The English Universities Press, Inc., gives the most complete and precise explanations and illustrations on the subject of pocketing a ball.

Number of Books	Source	Subject
64	England	Pocket billiards—English Losing and winning hazards combined with cannons (caroms)
1	India	Pocket billiards—English Losing and winning hazards combined with cannons (caroms)
9	United States of America	Pocket billiards—American
1	United States of America	Cushion billiards—American (Tables have no pockets)
1	France	Cushion billiards—French (Tables have no pockets)
2	Spain	Cushion billiards—Spanish (Tables have no pockets)
5	United States of America	Pocket billiards and cushion billiards—American
9	England	Snooker—English
1	South Africa	Snooker—English
8	England	Snooker and pocket billiards —English
1	England	Handbook and Constitution of The Women's Billiards Association, C/o Billiards Association and Control Council, 15, Exeter Street, London, W. C. 2.

14

A Few Words about Billiards English

When we talk about using billiards English most players think in the terms of striking the cue ball on either side, right or left, of its vertical axis. However, you impart English (spin) on the cue ball every time you strike it at a point that is off its *precise dead center.* You can verify this by placing the cue ball opposite Spot 17 and aiming it for Spot 8. Stroke carefully and hold the cue to see if you can make the cue ball bounce back and hit the tip of your cue. If it does not do that, then it is proof that you did not strike the cue ball at its dead center but must have struck it right or left of its vertical axis.

Therefore, the spot where the cue tip strikes the cue ball becomes very important; important, because English not only affects the cue ball but *also* imparts a spin (English) to the *object ball.*

When you strike the cue ball on its *right* side you are using *right English* which gives the cue ball a *counterclockwise spin.* The force of this spin throws the object ball to the *left* and at the same time imparts to the object ball a *clockwise* spin.

When you strike the cue ball on its *left* side you are using *left English* which gives the cue ball a *clockwise spin.* The force of this spin throws the object ball to the *right* and at the same time imparts to the object ball a *counterclockwise* spin.

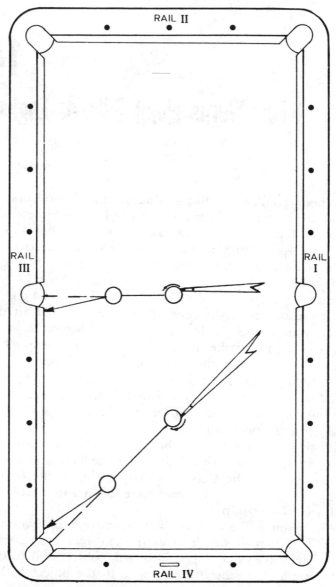

Diagram 15. Use of *un*intentional English.

This requires, that when you strike the cue ball on either side of its vertical axis, you must compensate by cutting your shot either a little more or a little less than you would when you play the shot straight-on, not using English.

If you are inattentive or careless and use right or left English without thus compensating, you will be surprised and baffled no end. Often your misses will occur unexpectedly and most aggravatingly on short easy shots. You will stand there and wonder what happened.

The use of unintentional right or left English is commonly overlooked or else is not understood, but it is vitally important. You can readily see that using English is a ticklish business. When English is imparted intentionally or unintentionally it is the cause of perhaps half of all shots that are missed. You might ask why is it used at all?

You use English only when it is absolutely necessary: A). to pocket the object ball or B). to position your cue ball for the next shot. Regarding the former situation, we can be thankful that in 80 to 90 percent of all shots the object ball can be pocketed by striking the cue ball right in the center. Regarding the latter, however, getting position on the next shot does not always come naturally.

When you cannot position the cue ball with the speed of your center-ball stroke alone, some kind of English is required; but it is advisable to use as little English as possible.

A few additional observations on the use of English:

1. If you have a straight-in shot to a pocket, your cue ball will not scratch if you use a little draw English.

2. On a *short* shot where you wish to use English to throw an object ball, impart a good spin to the cue ball and stroke *softly*, in order to give the cue ball a chance to throw the object ball into the pocket.

3. *The Big-Object-Ball-Target Technique.* On long distance shots it is difficult to cut (hit) the object ball at the precise contact point. When the cut is a slight one you can make the same shot by using a little English and then hitting the object ball *straight-on.* The advantage of using this latter method lies in the fact that you are close to the cue ball so you can be more accurate in striking it so as to give it the amount of English that you judge is necessary and thus it is easier to hit the object ball *straight-on;* whereas if you cut the object ball it is crucial that you hit it at the precise contact point called for. Obviously, hitting an object ball straight-on makes a *larger target* for you than when you are limited to hitting the object ball at the precise contact point, especially when the ball is many feet away from you and your cut has to be as small as $\frac{1}{8}$ or even thinner. In spite of the advantage of using this principle, some players prefer to cut the object ball *without* using any English.

The subject of the use of English is so complicated that much of the English language has to be used to explain the Billiards English. So, for the time being, take it easy and do not worry too much about the use of English. It will come naturally as you advance in playing ability. Reference to it will, of course, come up in future discussion. In the meantime here's a word of caution: use absolutely as little English in your playing as possible.

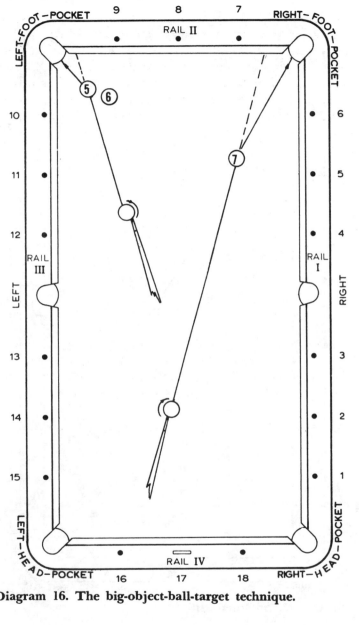

Diagram 16. The big-object-ball-target technique.

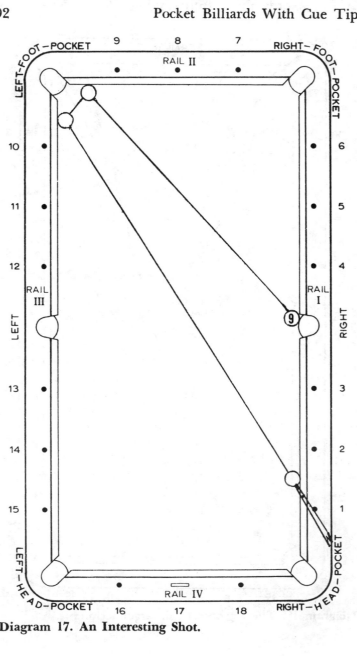

Diagram 17. An Interesting Shot.

15

Exercises: Three Interesting Shots

I show a shot that can be executed in three different ways on your home billiard table that will give the whole family a lot of fun. See Diagram No. 17.

Standing at Rail I of the table, with the cue ball between Spots 1 and 2, strike the cue ball moderately in the center and have it hit Rail III near the Left-Foot-Pocket. The cue ball then hits Rail II, bounces off and pockets ball 9 in the side pocket. (Your seven-year-old daughter can easily learn to make this shot.)

In Diagram 18 two object balls prevent dropping ball 9 in the side pocket in the same manner as shown in Diagram No. 17. Another way must be found:

Use right English (2 o'clock) and aim the cue ball for Rail II so it will just miss hitting ball 9. When the cue ball hits Rail II it bounces off, *reverses* its course and pockets ball 9 in the side pocket. (This shot is one for junior and Mom to try.)

With object balls preventing you from dropping ball 9 in the side pocket as shown in Diagrams 17 and 18, here is a third way of pocketing ball 9:

Use right English (2:00 or 2:30) and aim the cue ball to the point where the cushion and rail meet, as shown by the arrow, so the cue ball will bounce sufficiently

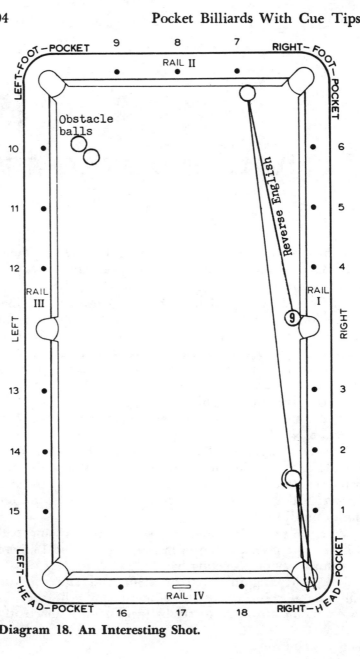

Diagram 18. An Interesting Shot.

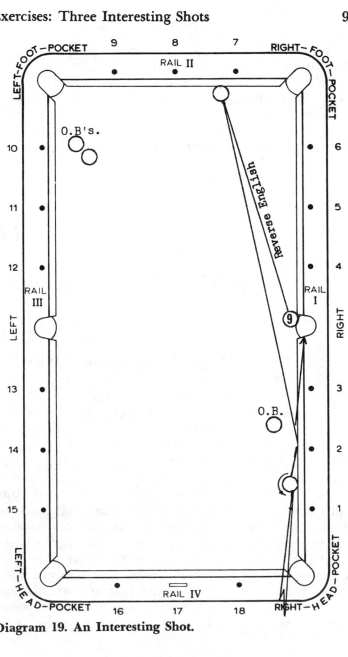

Diagram 19. An Interesting Shot.

far away from Rail I to miss hitting ball 9. The cue ball then continues on the remainder of its course as shown in Diagram No. 18 and pockets ball 9 in the side pocket. (This more difficult shot is for the young man of the house and Dad.)

In all of the above three cases, after pocketing ball 9 the cue ball will roll toward the head of the table.

16

The Long Angle and the Short Angle

To pocket an object ball there are three things that have to be done correctly:

1. The cue ball must be struck correctly.

2. The cue ball must hit the object ball correctly.

3. The object ball must be aimed for the proper side of the intended pocket correctly (unless, of course, you can make a perfect shot without the ball hitting either side of the pocket).

What is meant by the third point is that if an object ball has to enter a pocket from a slanting angle, it is not always easy to have it enter the pocket freely. It is therefore better to have your aim favor the side of the pocket farthest away from you (the side of the pocket that greets you, also referred to as the long angle). If it hits there, and your shot is a soft one, the ball will wobble back and forth and then has a chance to drop into the pocket.

But if the object ball hits the corner of the pocket

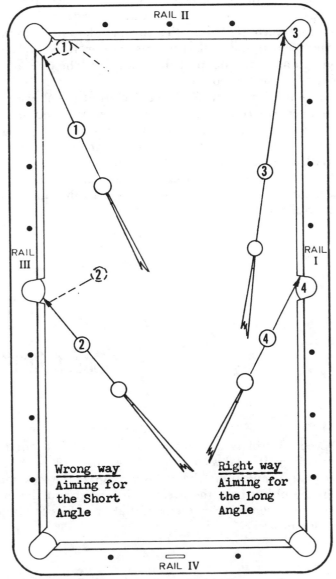

Diagram 20. The long angle and the short angle.

nearest you (the short angle), it will bounce away and
you will have a sure miss. In other words, the trouble-
maker of each pocket is the short-angle rail (cushion)
corner. When the ball hits this corner it is prevented
from going into the pocket. Therefore, beware of the
short angle of the pocket!

Naturally, while trying to execute all of the above three
maneuvers correctly, you must also keep in mind another
very, very important matter: is your cue ball going to
come to rest in a favorable spot for your next shot?

With earnest, concentrated, slow playing, one can gradually acquire the knack of natural cue ball control. In the
last analysis this is the one big answer to the question of
how to make high runs.

17

Speed Control

Speed control is a primary factor in pocket billiards,
especially as it relates to playing position.

In this connection, the greater degree the cut made
upon the object ball, the greater the speed and the more
difficult the control of the cue ball after it hits the object
ball. Examples:

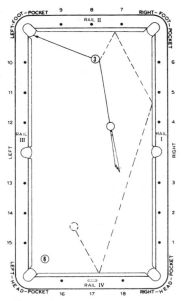

Diagram 21. Speed Control.

As opposed to

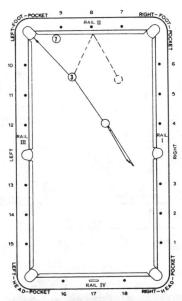

Diagram 22. Speed Control.

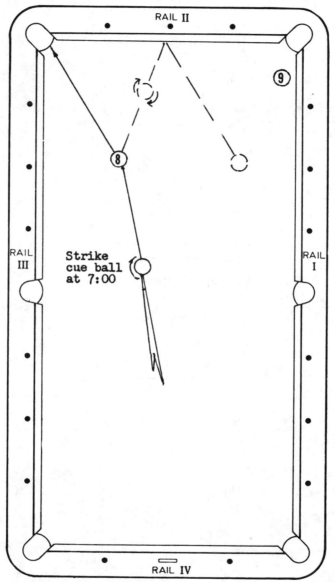

Diagram 23. Speed Control.

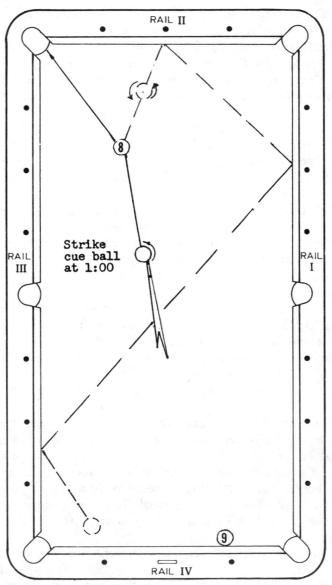

Diagram 24. Speed Control.

Conversely, a straight-in shot often (though not necessarily) finds the cue ball moving only a short distance after hitting the object ball, which can present problems in playing position on a ball some distance away.

More often than not, however, one finds oneself between these two extremes (as in Diagram 23) where the speed of the cue ball is crucial in playing position.

The speed is determined in two basic ways: first, by the force with which the cue ball is struck and, second, by the English imparted to the cue ball. Regarding the latter, a word of further clarification: after the cue ball hits the object ball and then hits a rail, the type of English on the cue ball determines to a significant degree the speed of the cue ball after bouncing from the rail. When hitting the rail, reverse English brakes the cue ball (Diagram 23) whereas non-reverse English (natural, running, or simple English) accelerates the speed of the cue ball (Diagram 24).

Speed control is a factor not only in playing position but also in executing certain shots. For instance, an angle shot into a side pocket has greater chances of falling if shot slowly or with a soft touch (Diagram 25).

Speed control in One Pocket, a game where each player must make balls only in one designated pocket: here a player often tries, especially on difficult shots, to hit the object ball with just enough force either to pocket it or at least to make it come to rest very near his designated pocket. Your ability to stroke the cue ball with just the right force can either make or break you. It can be the difference between being a mediocre or a good player.

Most players shoot too hard. However, you can also shoot *too soft* and when you do so three things can happen:

1. When your shot is not a straight one you can miss your shot because the object ball has a tendency to throw itself farther when you cut it with a soft stroke. Also, *un-*

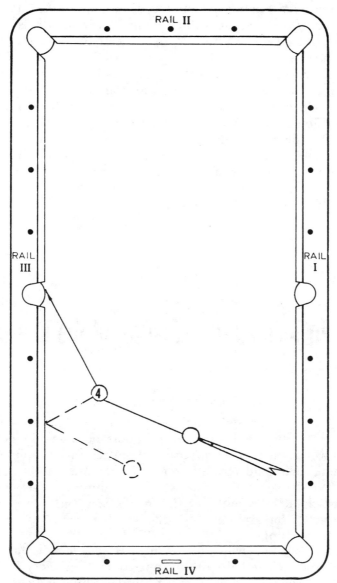

Diagram 25. Speed Control.

intentional English (when you do not strike the cue ball right at the precise center of its horizontal axis) has the same effect of throwing the object ball more one way or the other.

2. The cue ball hits the object ball with not enough force to propel it all the way into the pocket.

3. Shooting too softly can put the cue ball in a poor position as easily as stroking too hard.

On the whole, however, I like the advice of Willie Mosconi which is worth repeating: "the key words in billiard shotmaking are 'soft' and 'softer'."

18

Position Playing: Control of the Cue Ball

You read in books that practically every technique in playing billiards is very, very important. You commence to wonder if there is anything about learning to play the game that could possibly *not* be important.

Well, that is the way it is; you must do everything just right. Precision is of the first order; you cannot take any shot for granted, and that is what makes the game so fascinating.

Of one thing you can be sure: if you do not learn to control the cue ball you are not going to get very far.

You cannot expect to win by just pushing the cue ball

around the table, depending on luck to set up an easy next shot. Even if you are a good shotmaker, you must learn to set up each succeeding shot so that it is easy for you to make. Not learning cue ball control is like expecting to become a good musician without learning to read notes.

For instance, a partner of mine was recently forced to play a long difficult shot for the corner pocket. He made it and then, because of poor cue ball position, was forced to try another long difficult shot which he also made, but in doing so he got his cue ball in a tight spot again. Well, he was finished—made two fine shots and then was finished. That is not playing a winning game of pocket billiards.

Luther Lassiter and Cicero Murphy playing in a recent tournament seldom had hard shots to make for the simple reason that they positioned the cue ball after making each shot so that there usually was not more than one to three feet between the cue ball and the object ball.

Let us not forget that control of the force applied to the cue ball is a primary factor in mastering the art of position playing (see Chapter 17).

19

Coordination and Concentration

Irving Donald Crane—a study in concentration. Crane wound up winner of the 1968 World Pocket Billiards Championships.

Coordination is needed to pocket a ball and play position for the next shot. The principal reason a player falls apart in any sport or competition is that he loses his coordination, concentration, and often flies into a temporary outburst of temper as well.

If you are bothered by outside noises in a billiard room and miss an easy shot, you must control yourself, keep cool, and not panic. Forget the onlookers and concentrate. Attributes like these will prove the stuff of which you are made.

Does all this sound like hard work? Well, yes and no. As your game improves, you will be compensated with much joy and happiness. The sound of balls plopping into the pockets will sound to you as the harmonious notes of a Beethoven symphony sound to a true lover of music.

As there are many facets to a diamond, so also are there many facets to our superb game—more than those already mentioned in these chapters. There are bank shots, throw shots, combinations, caroms, and hundreds of fancy and trick shots.

Persons who wish to improve their playing ability should read available books on pocket billiards, then watch a professional or expert player in action and, if

Irving Donald Crane. *(National Bowlers Journal and Billiard Revue)*

possible, play with him, letting some of his lustre rub off
on you.

* * *

In making a comparison between the games of pocket
billiards and three-cushion billiards, you might say that
in pocket billiards accuracy is more important because
there is less margin for error; while in three-cushion billiards knowledge of the game is the paramount factor.

* * *

Reminders: Form your bridge tightly (meaning firm
not loose)

Hold your cue lightly (see Chapter 24 regarding the
forced draw shot)

Give your cue tip a few light strokes of chalk before
each shot. Never fail to take this precaution whenever
you stroke off center; otherwise you may miscue.

20

Exercises

Each player learns what kind of shots are the most
difficult for him to make. Therefore when he is at the
table alone, that is when he should try to improve on
his weaknesses.

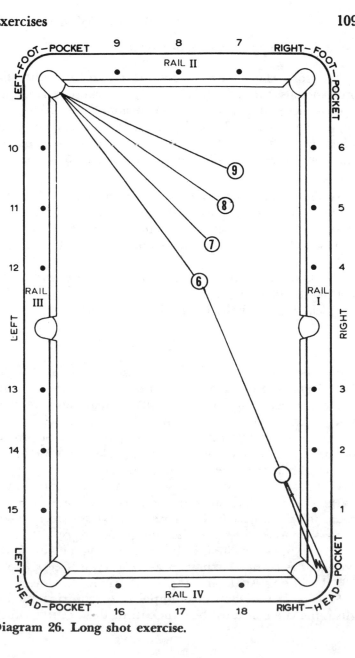

Diagram 26. Long shot exercise.

Long Shot Exercise

The long shots seem to give everyone, including the professionals, the most trouble. A good exercise is to put a tiny piece of paper near the head of the table, say, opposite Spots 1 or 2, placing the cue ball in front of it. Then place four to five balls on the right side of the table, in staggered fashion, opposite Spots 4, 5 and 6 (see Diagram 26).

With medium force and striking the cue ball in the center, try first to pocket the 6-ball in the Left-Foot-Pocket. If you miss, bring the cue ball back to the piece of paper and try the shot over and over until you make it.

Work on each of the other balls in the same way. Follow the same procedure on the other side of the table in pocketing the balls in the Right-Foot-Pocket.

Side Pocket Shot Exercise

Standing at the foot of the table, put seven balls against Rail I and the other eight against Rail III (where they are convenient for you to reach). Then improve your side-pocket shooting by placing the cue and object balls at different angles with respect to each other. Pocket all of the seven balls in the one side pocket and all of the eight balls in the other side pocket.

Ordinarily you use a soft stroke in making most shots to the side pocket. Some slanting shots leave barely enough room for the object ball to enter the pocket freely. With these shots one must exercise the greatest care:

First, your aim should favor the long angle of the pocket, the corner farthest away from you (see Chapter 16 "The Long Angle and the Short Angle") ;

Second, if the shot is a simple one requiring no English, the cue ball must be struck in its dead center, otherwise the object ball may be thrown to one side or the other (see Chapter 14, "A Few Words About Billiards English") ;

Third, players assume that a table is level. However, if you discover that it is not, then a moderate stroke, as opposed to a very soft one, will help to prevent the object ball running from off its course.

Give variety to your shots making some short, others long, some at difficult angles, with the cue ball sometimes against the rail. And do not forget to line up some of the shots perfectly straight because it is surprising how straight, easy shots can be missed.

In all these side pocket shots, stroke the cue ball exactly in the center. In many of the soft side-pocket shots, misses occur simply because the cue ball is not struck in the center. When you get off center you will observe, to your exasperation, the phenomenon of the effect of the use of *un*intentional English. No diagram is presented covering the above side-pocket exercises for the reason that they are so varied.

Draw Shot Exercises for Corner and Side Pockets

Now refer to Diagram 27 and develop your ability to position the cue ball after each shot by using the draw shot technique.

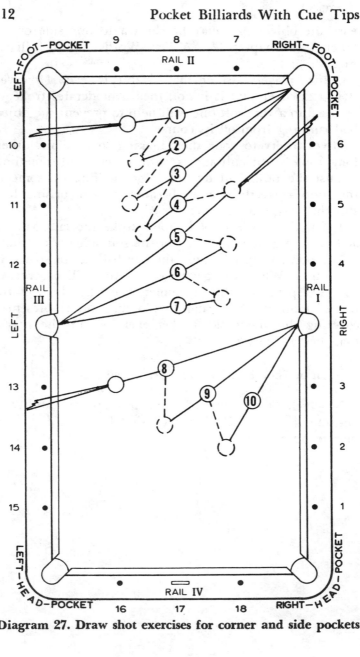

Diagram 27. Draw shot exercises for corner and side pockets.

21

The Throw Shot and the Kiss (Carom) Shot

Often two object balls, or the cue ball and an object ball, are frozen to or separated from each other by not more than a quarter of an inch. Pocketing one of them looks hopeless. With no playable shot in sight elsewhere on the table, an inexperienced player may then think he is finished. However, this need not be true. In such a situation the throw shot comes in handy. There are a number of ways to employ it:

Diagram 28-A shows how to throw ball 1, frozen to ball 2, into the Left-Foot-Pocket by making the cue ball hit the right side of object ball 2. The cue ball can be at different angles but you will still get the same result if you make the cue ball hit object ball 2 at this same contact point.

Diagram 28-B shows how to throw ball 3 into the Right-Foot-Pocket by a forced draw shot. Strike the cue ball at 6 o'clock, which gives it a strong underspin. This underspin has the effect of moving balls 3 and 4 forward so that the 3-ball will be in line with the pocket.

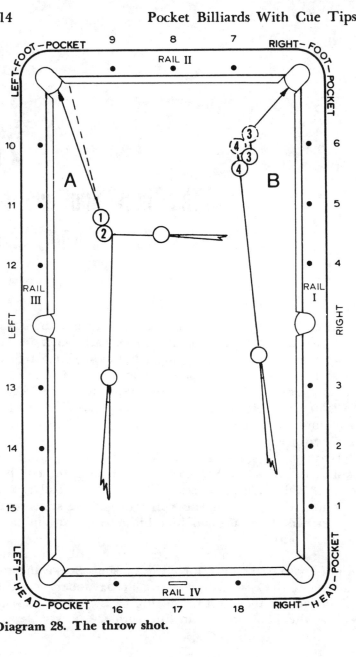

Diagram 28. The throw shot.

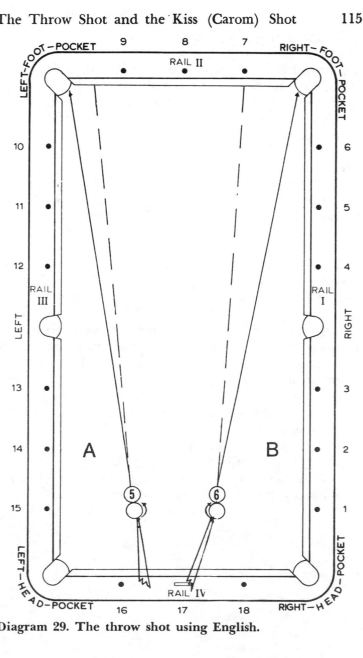

Diagram 29. The throw shot using English.

Diagram 29-A shows how to throw ball 5 into the Left-Foot-Pocket by using right English on the cue ball, stroking only hard enough to propel ball 5 into the pocket. The left spin given the cue ball makes the 5-ball spin to the right but in spite of this the 5-ball is thrown to the *left* because of the strong initial momentum the cue ball imparts.

Diagram 29-B shows how to throw an object ball (6) even farther by using both left English and aiming the cue ball in this case to Spots 4 or 5. I have experimented with these throw shots and, using a moderate stroke, just hard enough to pocket the ball, have been able to throw an object ball as much as 14 inches when using the whole length of the table.

Diagram 30-A shows how to throw ball 7 in the Right-Foot-Pocket. Place the tip of your cue against the cue ball at 9 o'clock and aim for Spots 4 or 5, then with *one* stroke of medium-soft force, ball 7 can be thrown as far as 30 inches into the pocket. This is a legal shot for the reason that the tip of the cue does not remain against the cue ball after starting your stroke. However, this extreme throw-off shot is not a practical one.

Diagram 30-B shows how to pocket ball 8 in the Left-Foot-Pocket. Place the tip of your cue against the cue ball at 1 o'clock, then slowly and carefully push the cue, forcing ball 8 into the pocket. Since the cue remains against the cue ball *after starting* your stroke, the shot is *not* considered a legal one. It is presented merely to show an interesting movement of the balls.

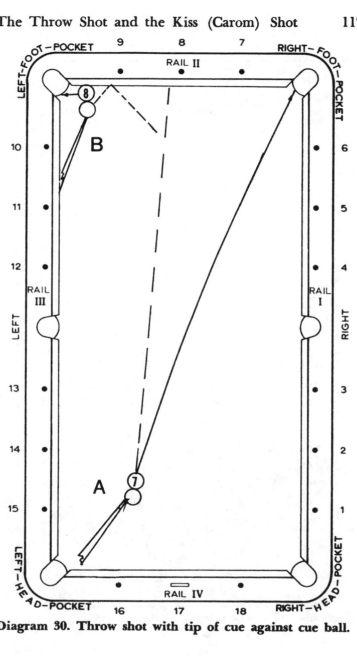

Diagram 30. Throw shot with tip of cue against cue ball.

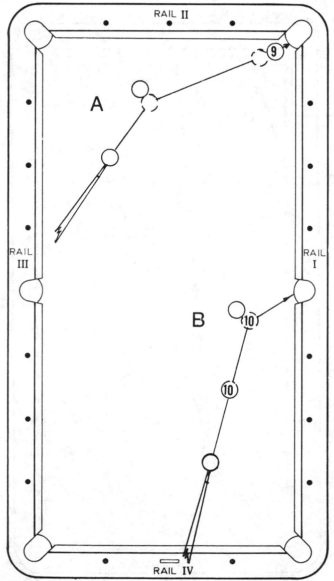

Diagram 31. The kiss (carom) shot.

A kiss shot (also called a carom shot) is another of the many interesting shots that play an important part in pocket billiards. It is made in two ways:

Diagram 31-A:

You call an object ball (in this case 9) to be dropped into the Right-Foot-Pocket and then have the cue ball hit one or more *other* object balls before it (the cue ball) hits the called object ball (9).

Diagram 31-B:

You call an object ball (in this case 10) to be dropped into the right side pocket and then have *that* object ball kiss one or more other balls before it (the called object ball) drops into the pocket designated.

By the way, any kiss shot (planned or accidental) counts provided the ball called drops into the pocket designated.

22
The Bank Shot

Making a bank shot is challenging but it is one of the Big Three (banks, combinations, and the use of English) that should be used only when it is to your advantage to do so or when you have no other alternative. Of all pocket billiard games, One Pocket requires by far the greatest bank-shot experience and ability from its players.

There are two kinds of bank shots: the easier (natural)

one that requires no English and the more difficult one that involves the use of English.

Plain Bank Shots (no English)

This shot can be easily explained and diagrammed. It requires that you aim and drive the object ball so that the *angle of incidence* to the banking rail *equals* the *angle of reflection* (the rebound angle) to the called pocket.

Draw lines as shown in Diagram 32. You will notice that the line from the cue ball and object ball to the banking rail and the path from the object ball to the pocket that it is to enter form a triangle of two equal lateral sides. The apex of the triangle is at Spot 11. Now if the cue ball were not in straight alignment with object ball 6 as shown, then, naturally, you would have to cut the object ball on one side or the other so as to have it hit Spot 11 and then bank into the Right-Foot-Pocket.

Then again, with the cue ball and object ball at different places than shown in Diagram 32-A, the apex of the triangle would not be at Spot 11 to carry out the isosceles-triangle principle.

When an object ball is frozen to a rail you must figure out what would form the correct triangle between the banking rail and the pocket of entry and then aim the cue ball to hit the precise contact point on the object ball (see Diagram 32-B). In making one of these bank shots, there is a tendency of the object ball as it rebounds from the rail to collide with the cue ball. To prevent this from happening, you must English the cue ball away from the direction in which the object ball is being banked. This English of course increases the angle of the rebounding object ball and you must, therefore, compensate for this by not cutting the object ball as much as you normally would.

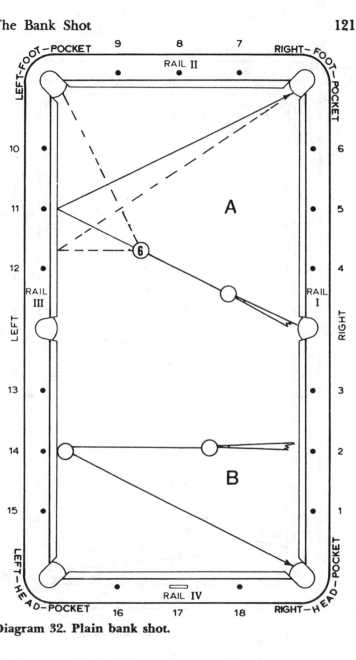

Diagram 32. Plain bank shot.

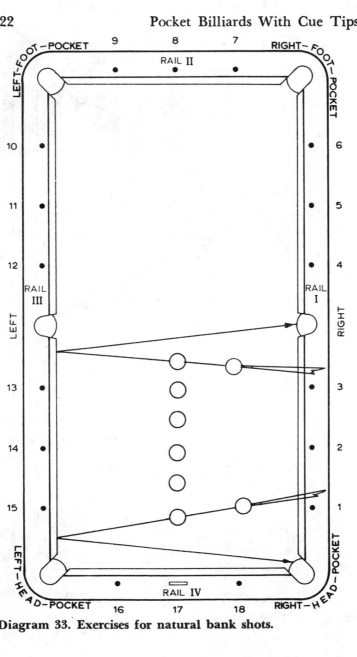

Diagram 33. Exercises for natural bank shots.

Diagram 33 shows exercises for learning to make natural bank shots. Line up all balls a few inches apart between Spots 8 and 17. Then bank them across the table into the corner and side pockets. Strike the cue ball in the center with medium force. Occasionally use both draw and follow as you would in regular play in order to get the cue ball position you desire.

Next in order would be to practice on the long difficult bank shots between the head and the end rails of the table.

Banking Shots Across the Table, Using English

When you employ English to execute a bank shot (because of obstructive balls or because you are trying for after-shot cue ball position), you may be in trouble. For instance to show what happens:

Using Left English. As explained in Chapter 14, left English throws the object ball to the right and makes that ball spin to the left (counterclockwise). This left spin as shown in Diagram 34:

A). Opens the angle from the first bank.

B). Closes the angle from the second bank and retards speed of ball.

C). Opens the angle from the third bank.

Using Right English. Right English throws the object ball to the left and makes that ball spin to the right (clockwise). This right spin:

A). Closes the angle from the first bank and retards speed of ball.

B). Opens the angle from the second bank.

C). Closes the angle from the third bank and retards speed of ball.

The object ball closes the angle and its speed is retarded when the spin of the ball is in opposition to the general direction in which the ball is rolling.

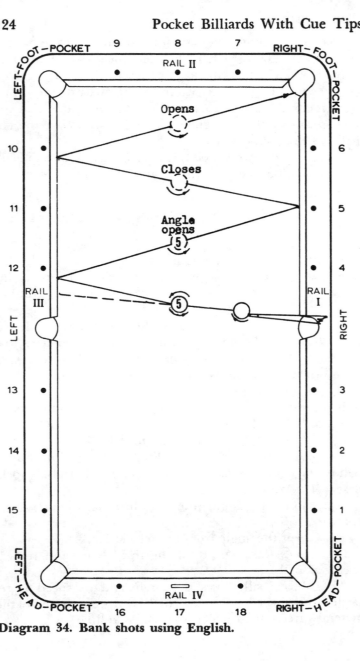

Diagram 34. Bank shots using English.

The object ball opens the angle when the spin of the ball is in harmony with the general direction in which the ball is rolling. (The expression *Running English* gets its name from this harmonious fast rolling action.)

Banking Shots Around the Table, Using English

When a spinning ball is banked around the table (see Diagram 35), you do not get angles that open and close as you do in across the table bank shots.

When a ball banked *around* the table hits the first cushion with running English, it continues with running English upon hitting all succeeding cushions. This is because the ball is spinning in harmony with the general direction in which the ball is rolling as it hits each cushion.

When a ball banked *around* the table hits the first cushion with reverse English it remains reverse English upon hitting all succeeding cushions. This is because the ball is spinning in opposition to the general direction in which the ball is rolling as it hits each cushion.

Reminder: the initial spin imparted to a ball, be it cue ball or object ball, remains the same until that ball comes to rest. We must remember that a spinning ball is itself affected and also produces certain effects as it hits other balls and the cushions.

You should practice on bank shots requiring English so that when you get stuck with one of them you will know what you are up against. Only practice, experience, and good judgment will help you figure out how much or how little English to use.

All Bank Shots

Striking the cue ball softly has the effect of opening the angle of travel of the object ball; striking hard closes

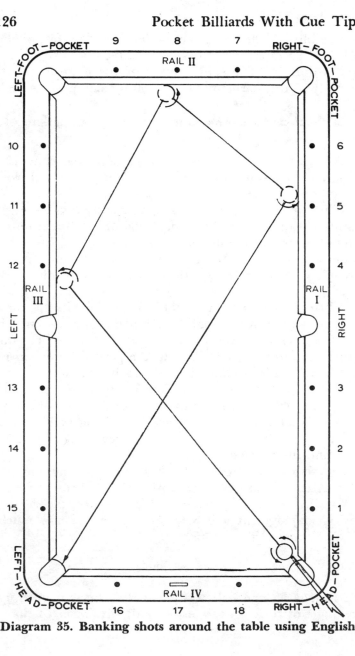

Diagram 35. Banking shots around the table using English.

the angle. A stroke of medium force on bank shots is recommended. (See also Chapter 14, "A Few Words about Billiards English.")

23

The Combination Shot

The combination is one of the Big Three shots (combinations, banks and the use of English) that should be used only when you have no other alternative. When you make combination shots though, they are things of beauty and can hardly be resisted. But they are dangerous—dangerous because they are most difficult and easily missed.

There are countless kinds of combinations, some that cannot be missed and others too difficult to attempt. Of course the one that is on or dead in is the one for which you can always safely go. It is one where two or more object balls are frozen to each other and in direct line with the opening of a pocket. In these shots all you have to do is to aim your cue ball to hit the contact point of the first object ball (see Diagram 36-A).

When balls frozen to or separated from each other by not more than 1/4 of an inch are slightly headed away from the pocket, they are still considered to be on. You can make this kind of a shot by having the cue ball hit a point on the first object ball so as to *throw* the balls one

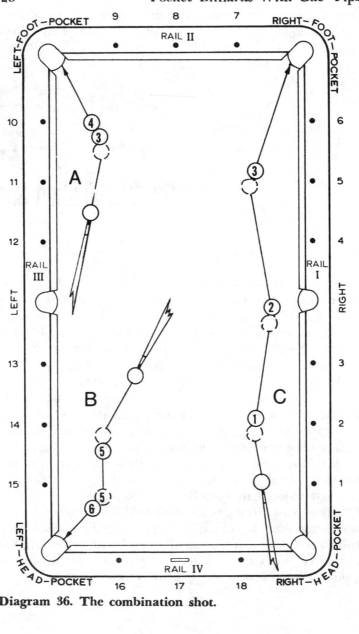

Diagram 36. The combination shot.

way or the other toward the pocket. Experience will teach you where to properly hit the first of the two or more object balls. (See also Chapter 21, "The Throw Shot.")

The fascinating combinations are the ones in which two or more object balls are separated from each other by *more than ¼ of an inch* and are not in line with the pocket. In such cases you have to make two or more calculations (see Diagram 36-B and C).

The string of three combinations, Diagram 36-C, is interesting but it is a theoretical, not a practical shot. It is presented merely to demonstrate the mechanics of the combination shot.

But beware! In playing natural combination shots (as with bank shots) you have to be extremely careful not to impart any English to the cue ball. The cue ball must be struck *precisely at its dead center*. Because this principle is difficult for some players to understand let me elaborate:

Suppose you unintentionally use left English as shown in Diagram 37-A. This makes the cue ball spin clockwise (to the right). When the cue ball hits ball 7, the force of this spin will naturally throw ball 7 slightly to the right. As a result the 7-ball will hit the 8-ball slightly on its right side making the 8-ball veer to the left toward Spot 10 instead of going directly into the Left-Foot-Pocket. The shot is missed if you use left English. If you strike the cue ball at its precise dead center instead, it would hit ball 7 straight-on and the 7-ball would hit ball 8 straight-on making it go into the Left-Foot-Pocket.

Diagram 37-B shows the mechanics of the same principle when you strike the cue ball on its right side.

In short, it is exceedingly difficult to make combination and bank shots when English becomes involved. The general and advisable rule is to look carefully for some easier shot before trying a combination or bank shot that you are not confident of making.

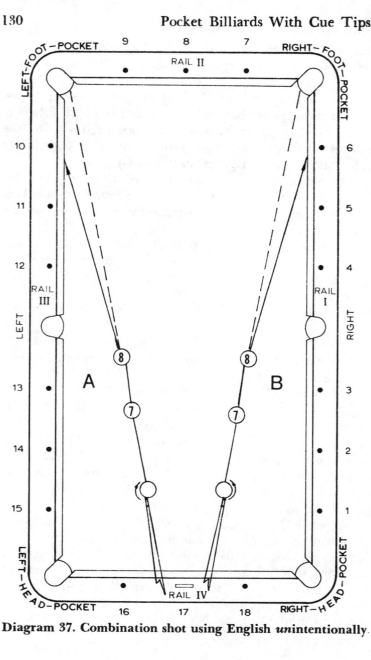

Diagram 37. Combination shot using English _unintentionally_.

24

Exercises: Center Ball, Draw, Follow, Stop and Near-Stop Shots

You should spend most of your practice time in mastering the center ball, draw, follow, stop, and near-stop shots—each, of course, with correct speed control. Improvement in these techniques automatically raises one's playing ability onto a higher plateau. The ability to draw the cue ball expertly will probably prove to be your most important asset. You must practice long and hard in these departments if you would hope to become a better-than-average player.

So, let's start in with the draw; it is the hardest to master. Form a short, low bridge. In doing this you may find it helpful to retract the middle finger so that it touches the palm of your hand (see photograph 15 in Chapter 4). Hold your cue handle low and level. Strike the cue ball as far below its horizontal axis as is safe without miscueing. Your stroke need not be a hard one. It should be firm, spring-like, and snappy but you do not pull your cue back; on the contrary it is very important that you *follow through* with the cue about four inches beyond the cue ball (see Diagram 1), in order to put added reverse, revolving motion (spin) on the cue

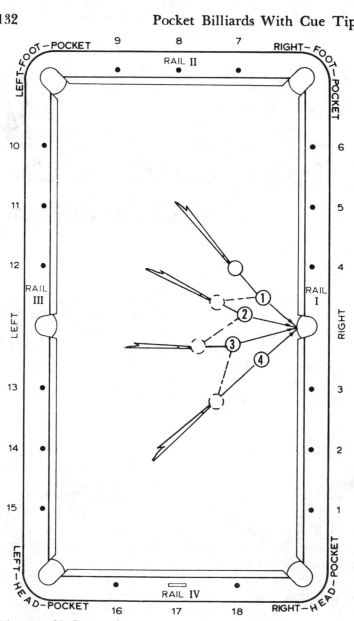

Diagram 38. Draw shot.

ball so that it will draw back toward you. This follow-through with the cue also helps to keep your stroke on a true course. On a forced draw shot, as for instance when the object ball is distant, you naturally have to stroke hard. Some players can make their draw shots effective by grabbing (clinching) the cue handle just before stroking. I prefer to grasp the cue handle firmly from the beginning to the end of the stroke.

Now place two balls, a few inches apart, about six inches away from the side pocket. With the cue ball a few inches farther back, pocket the closest ball and draw the cue ball so that it will slide behind the second object ball (see Diagram 38). This is more of a nip draw shot and requires but little force.

Next, place the balls farther away from the pocket and repeat your previous practice. After you have succeeded in developing these easy draw shots, you can practice pocketing and obtaining position with three, four, and more object balls.

Later on you will find it necessary to draw the cue ball with the use of right or left English as for instance when you want to draw back and have the cue ball hit one or more cushions, achieving the required position for your next shot (see Diagram 39). When you can execute these kinds of shots you are indeed stepping up and mingling with the advanced players.

Practicing with the follow shot (striking the cue ball above its horizontal axis) will be easier for you. Extreme care must be taken to apply a delicate touch to your stroke in order to control the distance the cue ball rolls after it hits the object ball (see Diagram 40).

A true stop shot (having the cue ball displace the object ball being hit) can be executed when the cue ball and the object ball are in straight alignment. You look through the center of both the cue ball and the object

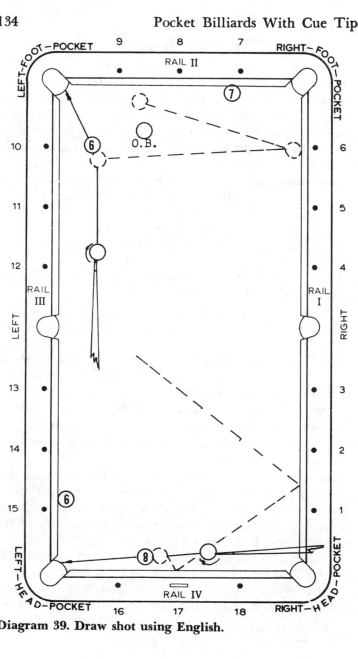

Diagram 39. Draw shot using English.

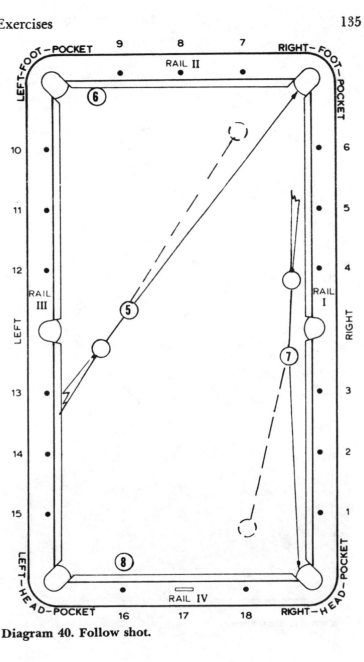

Diagram 40. Follow shot.

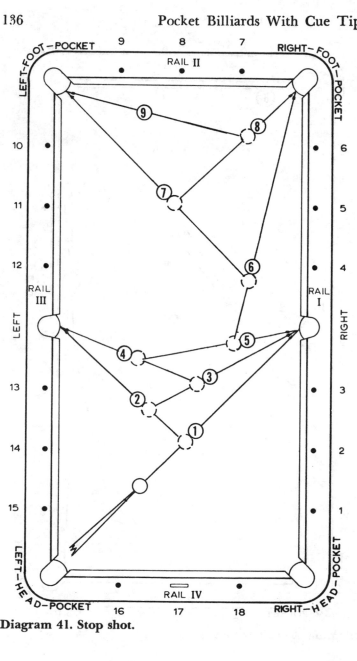

Diagram 41. Stop shot.

ball, then strike the cue ball at its dead center, having it hit the object ball straight-on with full impact. Referring to Diagram 41, this again is a theoretical set-up of balls. It is presented to show how useful the stop shot can be in acquiring position for your succeeding shot.

The near-stop shot is an extremely valuable one. Properly executed it leaves the cue ball in the vicinity of the object ball being pocketed, close to and in a favorable position for your next shot. It calls' for the use of most other strokes in that you can practically always make the cue ball either follow the hit object ball, or draw back or slide (swerve) to the right or to the left; this latter technique sometimes requires the use of a little English. To take momentum out of the cue ball you strike it lightly below center but you do not follow through with the cue as in a regular draw shot. One always tries to make the succeeding shot a short one, leaving the cue ball in as good a position as possible. This requires finesse and a delicate touch, which should make the near-stop shot a favorite one with the women players.

LEON YONDERS, *Cueing-Behind-Back Champion*

Watching an accomplished player skillfully executing the various shots covered in this chapter is a thing of beauty. The greatest expert of cue ball control, especially of the near-stop shot (also referred to as a slide shot), that I ever played with is Leon Yonders, now instructor at the new Palace Billiards, San Francisco. In January 1965, with witnesses present, he performed the amazing feat of pocketing 100 balls without a single miss, *without the cue ball touching any cushion,* and using the unorthodox style of playing with the cue behind his back for each of the 100 shots. (For each rack the 15 balls plus cue ball were haphazardly spread within the foot and middle areas of the table, none of the balls touching the cushions.)

Leon Yonders, Cueing-Behind-Back Champion. *(National Billiard News)*

Whether as a pupil or an opponent in a friendly game, you forget all about your turn to play as you watch in utter fascination how he strikes and controls the cue ball. It may be: (1) a follow shot he uses to pocket a ball and make the cue ball travel exactly the right distance, stopping by itself or by hitting another ball or a cluster of balls that need to be broken up; (2) a draw shot with or without English that makes the cue ball come to rest at an advantageous spot for the succeeding shot, or (3) a stop shot or near-stop shot that makes the cue ball "stick" or move only a slight distance upon contacting and pocketing an object ball. With masterful touch he wields his cue as Rembrandt his brush. Back in 1948 Yonders played with all the contemporary champions and received the compliments of the great Ralph Greenleaf.

25
POCKET BILLIARDS Is the Correct Name

When the author forwarded his first story to the *National Billiard News,* Philadelphia, which won first prize and was in the nature of an appeal for the initiation of a national campaign to urge the use of the correct name of our game, he said:

Who knows but that this story may some day prove to have been the turning point in relegating the poor-image word pool to the family of archaic words.

The *National Billiard News* published the story and its editor-publisher, Earl Newby, wrote:

> As soon as we reset your story on our stationery, we will mail copies to every one in billiards, like the BRPA, Brunswick Manufacturing, AM&F, Victor Billiards, Macon Billiards, National Billiards—a list that would take us too long to enumerate. We like your story very much. In the near future you will receive another bond. We of The *National Billiard News* staff appreciate a great billiard fan like you.
>
> Your Friend, (Sgd) Earl Newby.

It is quite understandable why many of our older people, through habit or carelessness, use the expressions pool and pool room. Many of the younger generation may not even know the correct names, but they will learn in time and take pride in using them. Take the bowlers, they no longer refer to the bowling alley but to the bowling lane.

What is incredible is to read in articles and to hear professional players still using the aforementioned old-fashion expressions. If they would only realize that every time they do this it hurts the sport. A game is what you make it. Choose to help our fine game by calling it by its dignified and correct name—*Pocket Billiards*.

Angels . . . Billiards, Quarles Emblems, c. 1634. (J. Mills, Printer, St. Augustine's Back, Bristol)

Louis XIV Plays Billiards, by Antoine Trouvain. (The Metropolitan Museum of Art, Whittelsey Fund, 1949)

Billiards. (The British Museum)

The Billiard Room, College Life. (The British Museum)

Le jeu de billiard, by L. Boilly. (Bibliotheque Royale de Belgique)

Championship match between John Deery and John McDevitt at Cooper Institute, New York, March 13, 1884 (Billiard Archives)

Billiards on a Liner, by S. Begg. The billiard table stabilizes itself automatically and remains level while the body of the table is well out of the plumb when the vessel is pitching. (The Mansell Collection, London)

Girl Standing on a Stool Playing Billiards, from Frank Leslie's
Illustrated Newspaper, April 7, 1884. (Billiard Archives)

Prince Tsuneyashi Takeda, the new president of the Nippon
Billiard Association, president of Japanese Olympic Committee, member of International Olympic Committee, vice-presi-
dent of the Union Mondiale de Billiard. *(Le Billard—Bulletin
L'Union et de la Confederation de Billard)*

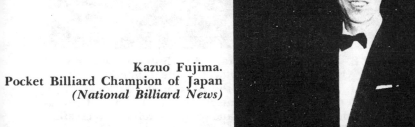

Kazuo Fujima.
Pocket Billiard Champion of Japan
(National Billiard News)

Robert E. Froeschle, consultant for Billiard Congress of America, chairman of the Official Rule Committee of the BCA, tournament director of the BCA, past director of Association of College Unions Intercollegiate Billiard Tournament for the past ten years and now its referee, recreation manager of Iowa Memorial Union.

Joe Balsis, Pocket Billiards Champion. *(National Bowling Journal and Billiard Revue)*

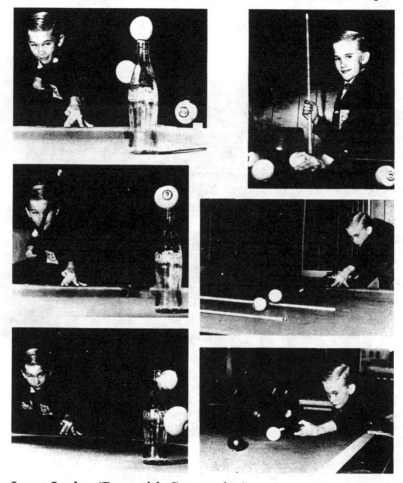

Larry Leake. (Brunswick Corporation)

Part 2

26
Cue Tips

How can a player advance beyond his class? I avail myself of this last opportunity to again stress the evident importance, yes necessity, of acquiring the ability to control the cue ball in order to have each succeeding shot playable and as easy to make as possible. This requires knowledge and experience with respect to three things:

First, you must know how the cue ball will behave after it is struck with the tip of your cue (refer. to Chapters 12 and 14).

Second, you must know just how much force to use in striking the cue ball (refer to Chapter 17).

Third, you must use good judgment, extending your horizon beyond the immediate shot to *at least* one position-play ahead (refer to Chapter 18).

After the rack is broken and during play, the balls can roll and group themselves into thousands of different clusters and positions with relation to each other.

Some players seem to be born with the knack of controlling the cue ball but with others it comes only with difficulty, requiring much practice, experience, and patience.

*   *   *

You are now invited to examine the following group

of diagrams. This is an evolutionary feature—invention—that may indeed prove to be the most important part of this book. By studying and practicing these shots a player should improve his ability to make higher runs. Experiment and try them over and over. Remember, pocket billiards is a precise and scientific game that requires practice and more practice, plus concentration, determination, and patience.

GOOD LUCK!

The diagrams shown in Part 2 cover:

A). Position-play studies of lies or patterns of balls on the table with explanations (CUE TIPS) as to how, with cue ball control, you can plan two, three, and more position-plays ahead so as to increase your run of balls.

B). Practical instructive shots.

C). Miscellaneous and interesting shots, some with balls preset. In some instances you have the choice of using either the draw or follow technique. You should use the one in which you excel. Other shots call for the use of various kinds of English.

Summary of Diagrams

Group Kind	Diagram Numbers
General Position	42 to 48
14.1 Continuous	49 to 58
One Pocket	59 to 62
Eight Ball	63, 64, and 65
Nine Ball	66, 67, and 68
Line Up	69 to 74
Rotation	75, 76, and 77
Miscellaneous	78 to 88
Snooker	87 and 88

Note: In the diagrams, I have given the object balls consecutive numbers in order to help you follow the order of shooting.

When reading each explanation be sure that the diagram number is the same as the one at the bottom of the diagram to which it relates.

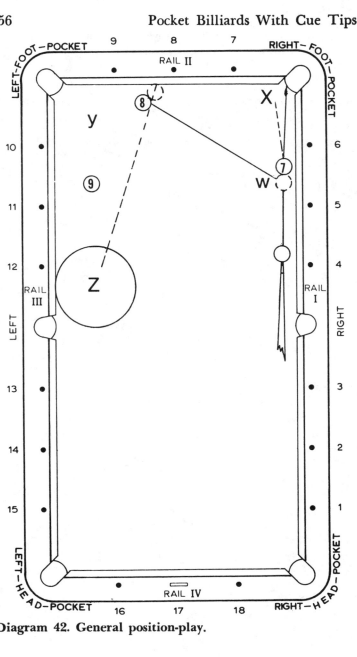

Diagram 42. General position-play.

Diagram 42—General Position-Play

Position play is not concerned with merely playing position on the next ball, but often on two and more balls ahead. Here is a simple example. One should pocket the 7-ball in the Right-Foot-Pocket, striking the cue ball in such a way that it sticks (neither following through nor drawing back) at position W. This way you have not only an easy shot on the 8-ball but you are ideally situated to play position on the 9-ball. Among beginners the temptation here is to get too good of position on the 8-ball by having the cue ball follow through to position X. Although the shot on the 8-ball then becomes very easy, the position-play on the 9-ball is not so easy. True, one can simply make the 8-ball and follow through to position Y with the cue ball; then pocket the 9-ball in the Left-Head-Pocket. But if your cue ball winds up two or three inches away from position Y, then the 9-ball shot to the Left-Head-Pocket is a difficult one. On the other hand, when shooting at the 8-ball from position W the cue ball will be in a good position for the 9-ball anywhere within the circle-area Z.

Diagram 43—General Position-Play

Situation: the opponent made the 6-ball but scratched (cue ball was pocketed accidentally). Now the 6-ball is spotted and you have the cue ball in (your) hand to place at your choosing behind the head string.

CUE TIPS: In order to play position on the 7-ball you place the cue ball behind the head string and as far right as possible without making your bridge uncomfortable. Now you may choose between one of two shots: (A) Stroke the cue ball with a soft touch so that it hits the 6-ball with just enough force to drive it into the Left-Foot-

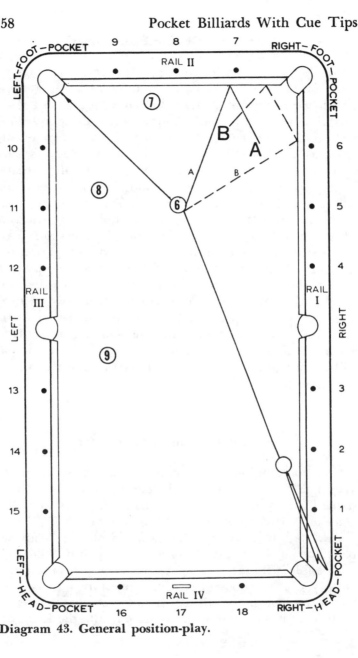

Diagram 43. General position-play.

Pocket. The cue ball should then stop at about position A which is good position on the 7-ball and an ideal place to play position on the 8-ball. (B) Strike the cue ball at 5 o'clock with force enough to draw it back after hitting the 6-ball into the Left-Foot-Pocket. This way you should avoid scratching the cue ball in the Right-Foot-Pocket and have excellent position on the 7-ball at position B. Note here, when the cue ball hits Rail 1 it will be spinning somewhat counterclockwise, which tends to break the speed of the cue ball in view of the angle at which it is approaching that rail.

The crucial matter in shot (A) is that you strike the cue ball with a soft touch so that it does not rebound off Rail II with such force that it ends so far up the table you no longer are in a position to pocket the 7-ball.

The crucial matter in (B) is that you strike the cue ball with sufficient draw English to prevent from scratching in the Right-Foot-Pocket, whereby the cue ball, after hitting ball 6 into the Left-Foot-Pocket, hits *first* Rail 1 and then afterwards perhaps Rail II.

Which of these two position shots is better?

Answer: the one that is the easiest for the player!

Among good billiardists this is invariably shot (B). He will have no difficulty in avoiding the possible scratch. On the other hand, the beginner may find shot (A) less difficult. However, once a player learns how to draw the cue ball *at long range,* that is, when the cue ball must travel some distance before hitting the object ball, shot (B) should surely be his choice.

The application of this position-shot play appears often, not just when the object ball is on the foot spot, the player has the cue ball in hand, and the next object ball is near end Rail II.

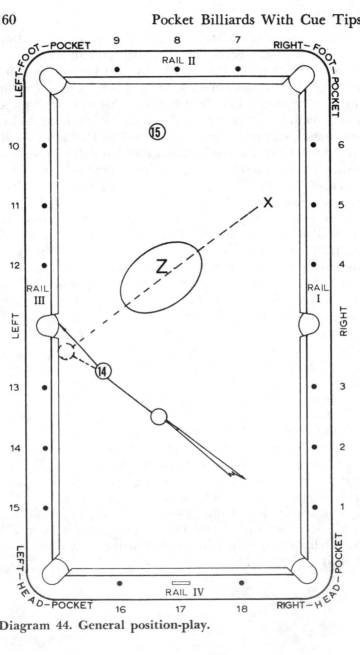

Diagram 44. General position-play.

Diagram 44—General Position-Play

Situation: the 14-ball is lying just a fraction *left* of being straight-in to the side pocket. To play position on the 15-ball, strike the cue ball at 1 o'clock with a smooth follow-through stroke of medium force. This should get the cue ball in the vicinity of X. On position plays of this nature, it is better to follow through beyond Area Z or short of Area Z because it is, perhaps, the worst area on the table from which to make the 15-ball: (1) you will have to stretch or use the bridge to reach the cue ball; and (2) you will have to bank the 15-ball to the far distant Head-Pocket.

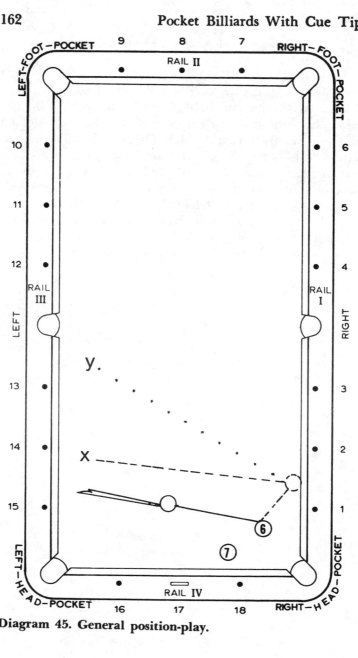

Diagram 45. General position-play.

Diagram 45—General Position-Play

In order to reach position X strike the cue ball at 2 o'clock with somewhat less than medium force. Should the cue ball be struck with no English, it would go in the direction of Y and might even scratch in the side pocket. In using reverse English, one should aim to hit the object ball (6) thinner than usual, since in this case the reverse English required to keep the cue ball in position for the 7-ball tends to throw the object ball (6) to the left of the pocket.

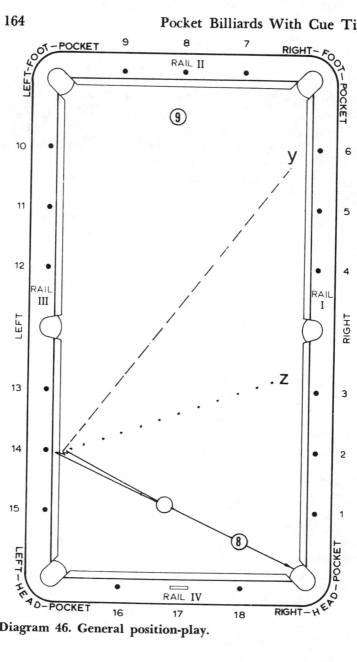

Diagram 46. General position-play.

Diagram 46—General Position-Play

Situation: the cue ball, the 8-ball, and the Right-Head-Pocket are in a perfectly straight line (that is, a straight-in shot). To be sure, the shot is very easy but position-play on the 9-ball is not—at least not for the amateur. Draw your cue ball with considerable force, striking it at 5 o'clock. This should get your cue ball in the vicinity of Y. But if you simply draw your cue ball, striking it at 6 o'clock, it will end up at or near position Z.

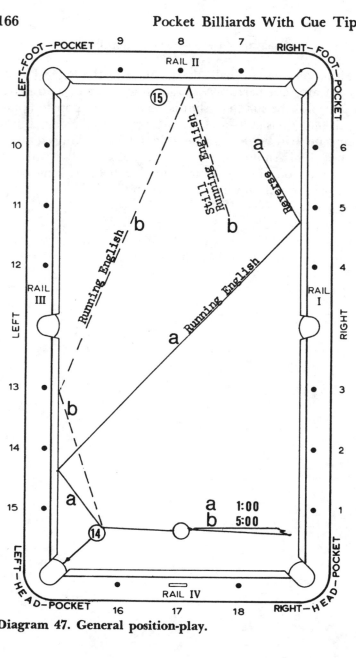

Diagram 47. General position-play.

Diagram 47—General Position-Play

Here is a simple position-shot on ball 15 that can be made in two ways. But one is considerably better; namely, the one shown by the solid line, Shot A.

In Shot A (solid line) you strike the cue ball at 1 o'clock and impart follow English. But being a bank shot *across* the table, running action of the cue ball becomes reverse action upon hitting Rail I, which tends to slow up the speed of the ball!

In Shot B (broken line) you strike the cue ball at 5 o'clock and impart draw English that carries the cue ball farther up Rail III than in the previous shot and then to Rail II. Now note this: when the cue ball hits Rail II it becomes a bank shot *around* the table and therefore the speed of the cue ball does not slow up when it hits that rail. True it was struck with draw effect at 5 o'clock but this draw was *railwise* (running harmoniously with Rails III and II), thus it keeps on rolling that way around the table until it comes to rest.

In short, the resting spot of the cue ball can be better controlled in Shot A. In Shot B the resting spot is less predictable because of the railwise running action of the cue ball. (See Chapter 22, "The Bank Shot.")

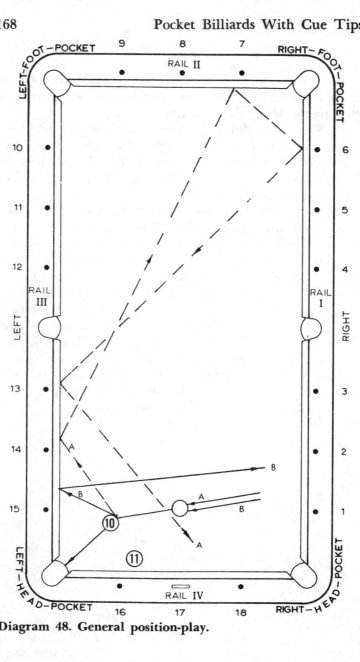

Diagram 48. General position-play.

Diagram 48—General Position-Play

There are two ways to play position here. First, play around the table noted in broken line (A). Strike the cue ball between 4 and 5 o'clock with considerable force. In this case you must make certain that after the cue ball hits Rail III, it must then hit Rail II and not Rail I. And second, noted in solid line (B), strike the cue ball at 10 o'clock with medium force (reverse English). The advantage of this shot lies in the fact that a scratch is less likely, and you have a shorter distance for the cue ball to travel in getting position on ball 11.

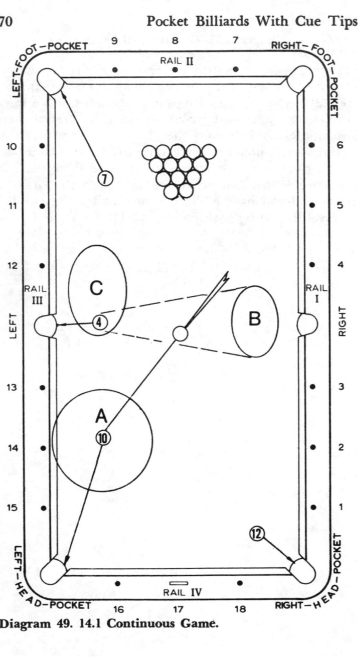

Diagram 49. 14.1 Continuous Game.

Diagram 49—14.1 Continuous or 14.1 Straight
Pocket Billiards

Key Ball and Break Shot. Naturally the 7-ball lies in the best position for a break shot. Next, the 4-ball (key ball) lies in the best spot to play the position you want on the 7-ball for the break shot. Actually the key here is to get as straight in on the 4-ball as you can (note cone B at the right side pocket).

Therefore pocket first the 10-ball, keeping the cue ball in or near circle A after the shot. Next, pocket the 12-ball in such a way (depending upon its position after the 10-ball shot) as to drive the cue ball into the cone area B. Then pocket the 4-ball, leaving the cue ball in area C, an ideal position for the break shot off the 7-ball.

In the 14.1 game, position-play, especially on the break shot and the key shot leading up to it, is essential.

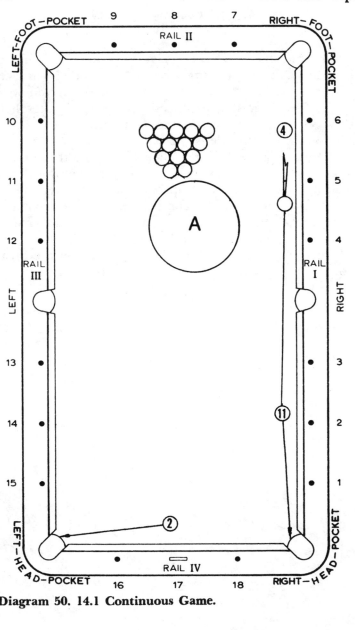

Diagram 50. 14.1 Continuous Game.

Diagram 50—14.1 Continuous Game

The temptation is to play the 4-ball, which is, to be sure, the easiest shot. However the 4-ball is, by far, in the best position for a break shot. Therefore the more professional approach here would be to first pocket the 11-ball and then the 2-ball so that the cue ball comes to a halt in circle A.

Diagram 51—14.1 Continuous Game

Here again the temptation is to make the 1-ball first since this shot is so easy because of the lie of the cue ball. However the 1-ball is far and away the best break shot. Therefore pocket first the 4-ball. Here the cue ball should bounce off Rail II to the head end of the table. This should make the 7-ball shot in the Left-Head-Pocket quite easy, after which the cue ball should stop within the circle. If the cue ball should stop in part A of the circle, then draw-English should be used in making ball 1 on the break shot in order to avoid scratching the cue ball off the rack into the Left-Foot-Pocket.

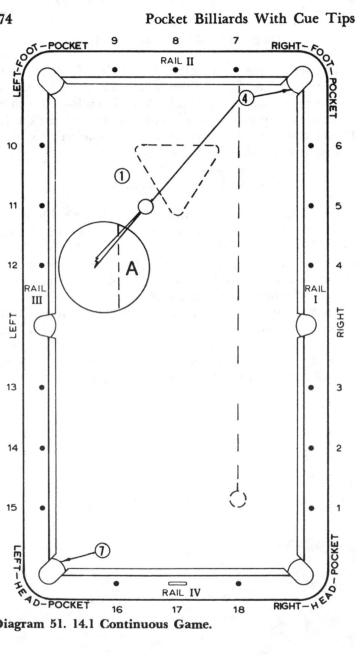

Diagram 51. 14.1 Continuous Game.

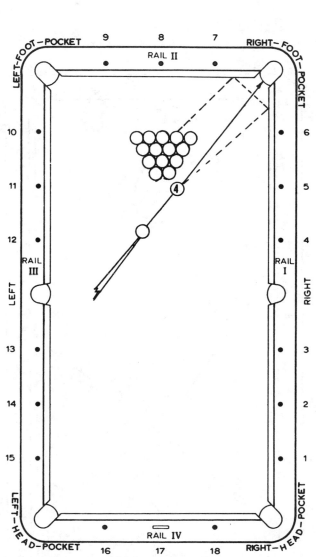

Diagram 52. 14.1 Continuous Game Break Shot

Diagram 52—14.1 Continuous Game Break Shot

This is a challenging break shot. You pocket the 4-ball using very slight English so as to have the cue ball hit Rail I. An option here would be the safe shot, namely, pocket the 4-ball and draw the cue ball back to the end rail, calling for a safe shot, in advance to be sure.

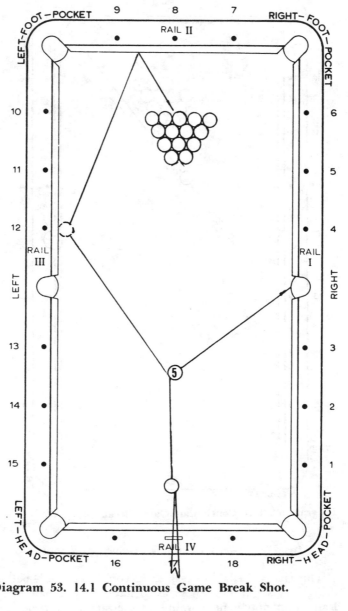

Diagram 53. 14.1 Continuous Game Break Shot.

Diagram 53—14.1 Continuous Game Break Shot

In the 14.1 Continuous game you must be prepared to execute break shots that are not always ideal. Diagram 53 is one of these. The cut required on the 5-ball for the right side pocket is somewhat crucial. Also, you must use running right English (strike the cue ball at 2 o'clock) with enough force to propel the cue ball from Rail III to Rail II and then into the rack of balls. If the player considers the shot too difficult to attempt then playing safe could be done in a variety of ways, one being to shoot the shot as diagrammed but with no intention of making the 5-ball and with such force as to simply leave the cue ball behind the rack of balls.

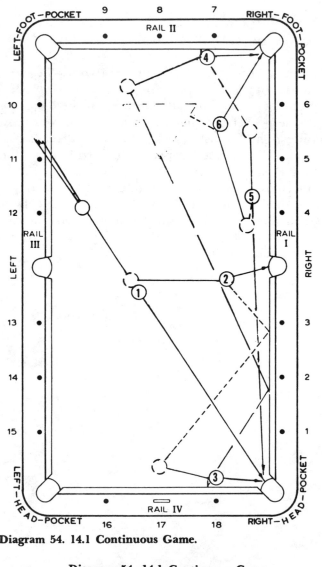

Diagram 54. 14.1 Continuous Game.

Diagram 54—14.1 Continuous Game

Ball No.	How to Strike the Cue Ball
1	Center; firm, medium force
2	Right, soft
3	9 o'clock, hard
4	3 o'clock, soft
5	Slight follow
6	Center, hard

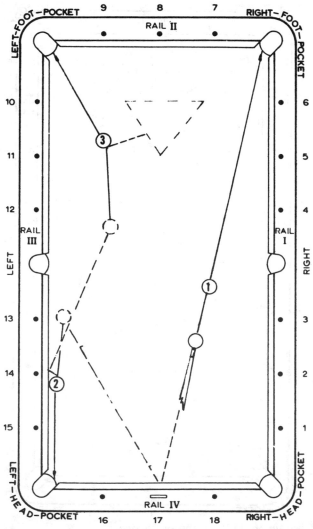

Diagram 55. 14.1 Continuous Game.

Diagram 55—14.1 Continuous Game

Ball No.	How to Strike the Cue Ball
1	6 o'clock, forced draw
2	6 o'clock, forced draw
3	Center, hard

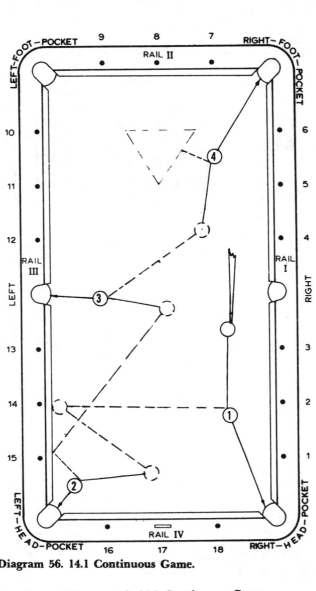

Diagram 56. 14.1 Continuous Game.

Diagram 56—14.1 Continuous Game

Ball No.	How to Strike the Cue Ball
1	7 o'clock, medium
2	6 o'clock
3	6 o'clock
4	Center, hard

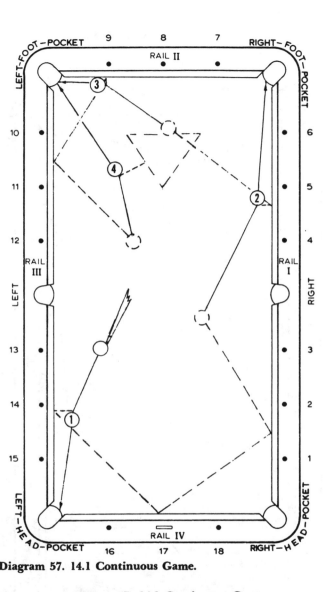

Diagram 57. 14.1 Continuous Game.

Diagram 57—14.1 Continuous Game

Ball No.	How to Strike the Cue Ball
1	9 o'clock. Or you could get the cue ball at the same position by cueing at 3 o'clock, slight draw
2	10 o'clock, soft
3	10 or 11 o'clock
4	Center, hard

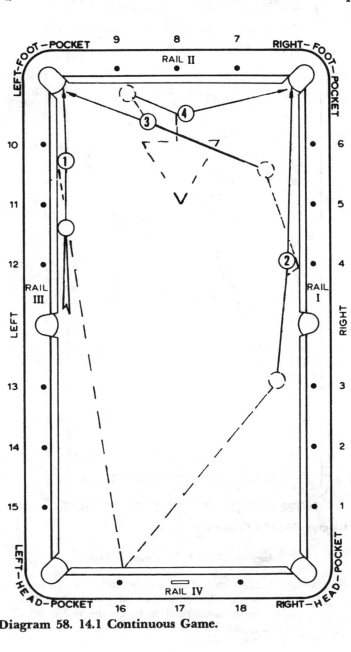

Diagram 58. 14.1 Continuous Game.

Diagram 58—14.1 Continuous Game

Ball No.	*How to Strike the Cue Ball*
1	7 o'clock, forced draw
2	Center, soft
3	Center
4	Center, hard

Diagram 59—One Pocket Game

In One Pocket one player has the Right-Foot-Pocket and the other the Left-Foot-Pocket. Let us say you have the Left-Foot-Pocket and you are to shoot first.

There are three possible shots (see Diagrams 59, 60, and 61). Here is the first:

Place the cue ball as indicated. Strike the cue ball at 10 or 11 o'clock with medium force (that is, with good English). Hit the head ball (in this case the 1-ball) thinly on the right. The cue ball should then stop within or near circle A. None of the broken racked balls should be in position for your opponent to play in the Right-Foot-Pocket, while three or four balls should rest in the vicinity of your pocket. Your opponent is now forced to play safe and is on the defensive.

Diagram 60—One Pocket Game

The play is break shot number two. Once again you have the Left-Foot-Pocket and the opening shot. Strike the cue ball dead center lightly and hit the head ball (the 1-ball) full in the face or ever-so-lightly to the right, so the cue ball rests in circle A after the shot. The 2-ball should then stop in the vicinity of circle B. Balls 4, 5, 6 and 7 should hardly move from their original position. Thus your opponent is forced to play a very difficult safety. The unfortunate aspect of this break shot compared to the first break shot noted (see Diagram 59) is that you have put essentially only one ball, not three or four, in the vicinity of your pocket.

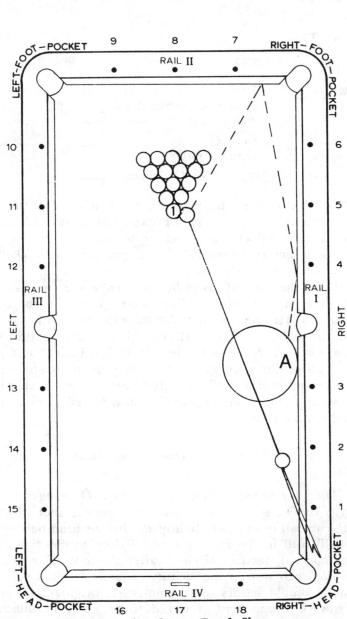

Diagram 59. One Pocket Game; Break Shot.

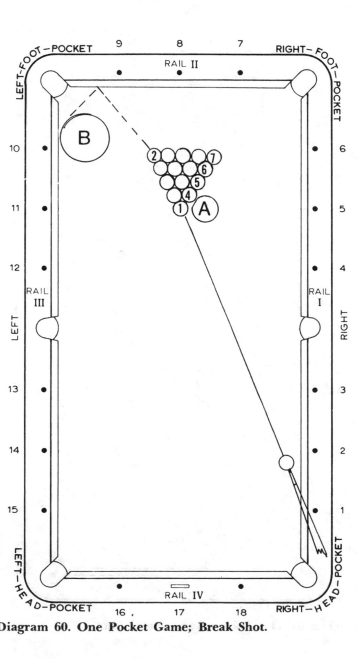

Diagram 60. One Pocket Game; Break Shot.

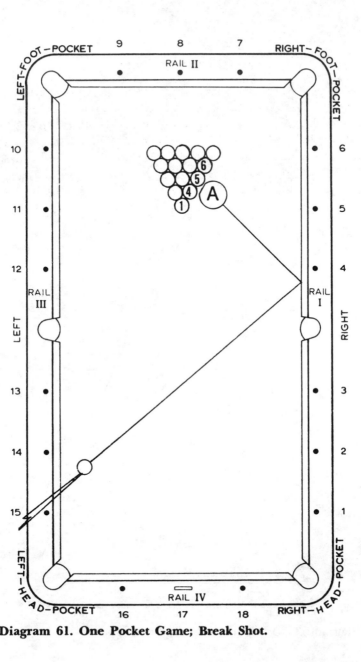

Diagram 61. One Pocket Game; Break Shot.

Diagram 61—One Pocket

The play is break shot number three. Here is the third and least advisable break shot in the One Pocket game, because it is the most risky. Strike the cue ball at 3 o'clock with medium force so it hits spot 4 and then the racked balls 4, 5, or 6 (preferably 5). The cue ball should stop in circle A. Several balls should now be in the vicinity of your pocket, the Left-Foot-Pocket, and no balls (if you are fortunate) in the vicinity of the Right-Foot-Pocket.

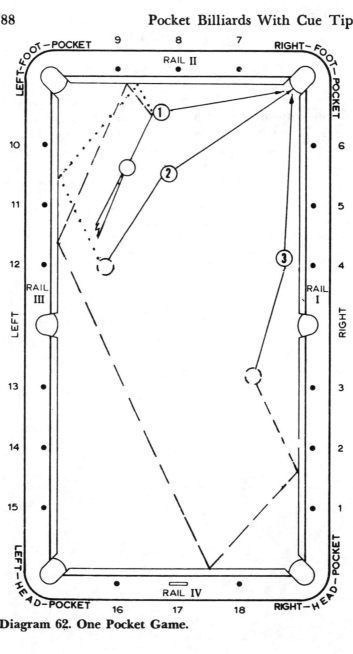

Diagram 62. One Pocket Game.

Diagram 62—One Pocket Game

The cardinal principle in playing One Pocket is the safe shot. This even applies when trying to pocket a ball that can be easily missed. In such a situation one plays a safe position against the opponent in case he misses his own shot.

In Diagram 62 the dashed lines illustrate how *not* to play position from ball 1 since, if one misses the shot, the opponent then has a shot on ball 2 into his Left-Foot-Pocket. A better and safer shot would be to strike the cue ball lightly at 7 o'clock cutting the 1-ball into your Right-Foot-Pocket and making the cue ball play position on the 2-ball (see dotted lines). This way, if you should miss the 1-ball, you will leave your opponent safe.

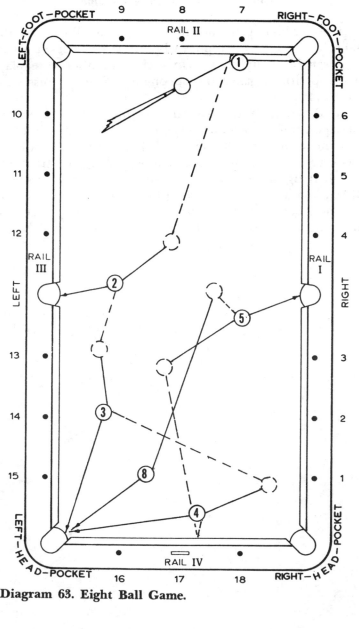

Diagram 63. Eight Ball Game.

Diagram 63—Eight Ball Game

Ball No.	How to Strike the Cue Ball
1	6 o'clock, medium soft
2	Center, soft
3	6 o'clock, soft
4	6 o'clock
5	6 o'clock, nip draw
8	Winning ball

Diagram 64—Eight Ball Game

Ball No.	How to Strike the Cue Ball
1	Center
2	Center
3	Follow
4	Center
5	Center
6	Center
7	Follow, soft stroke hitting the cushion first
8	3 o'clock, right English hitting the cushion first slightly behind the 8-ball.

Shot 7 is not an easy one unless the 7-ball is closer to the pocket. It is presented as an informative shot and one that will prevent the cue ball from scratching.

Diagram 65—Eight Ball Game

Ball No.	How to Strike the Cue Ball
4	5 o'clock
5	11 o'clock, soft
6	6 o'clock; nip draw
7	Follow
8	Winning ball. Here is a thorny finish shot

because ball 12 does not give you enough room to correctly cut ball 8. Shoot straight, hitting ball 8 straight-on. But you then must use good right English at 3 o'clock. Stroke very softly so that the 8-ball will have time to be thrown into the pocket by the spin of the cue ball.

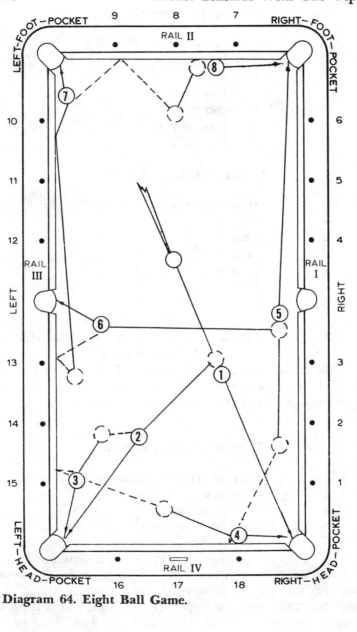

Diagram 64. Eight Ball Game.

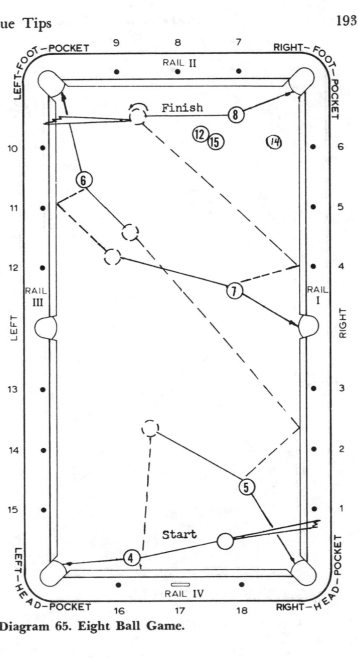

Diagram 65. Eight Ball Game.

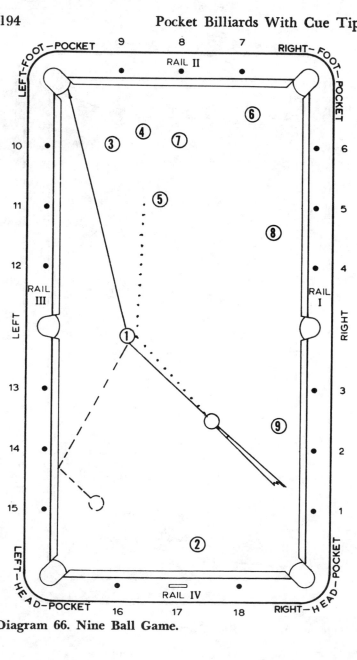

Diagram 66. Nine Ball Game.

Diagram 66—Nine Ball Game

The game is Nine Ball, the winner being the one who pockets the 9-ball. Only the unknowledgeable beginner would execute the easy shot of pocketing the 1-ball in the side pocket since position on the 2-ball is then virtually impossible except by pure luck. Since one gains nothing in this game by making the 1-ball, one must select the shot that will at least give one position on the 2-ball in hopes of running out. Therefore the 1-ball should be made in the *Left-Foot-Pocket* by putting a slight draw on the cue ball. To have the cue ball stop near *spot* 15 is not crucial. *Nearly* any area at the head end of the table would be satisfactory. The crucial matter here is the shot itself, pocketing the 1-ball.

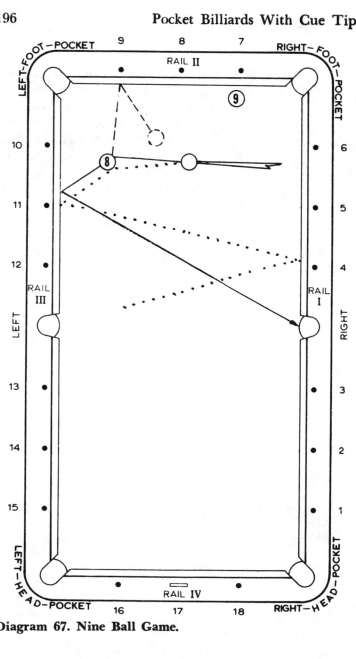

Diagram 67. Nine Ball Game.

Diagram 67—Nine Ball

The 8-ball can be cut into the Left-Foot-Pocket, but this shot should not be attempted for two reasons: (1) the cue ball may scratch in one of the side pockets and (2) it is unlikely that the cue ball will be in a position to make the 9-ball after the shot. You should attempt to bank the 8-ball in the Right-Side-Pocket, which will (a) leave your cue ball in a good position to make the 9-ball and (b) leave your opponent in a difficult position to shoot at the 8-ball if you should miss it on the bank shot. When banking the 8-ball, strike the cue ball at 5 o'clock with a medium force draw.

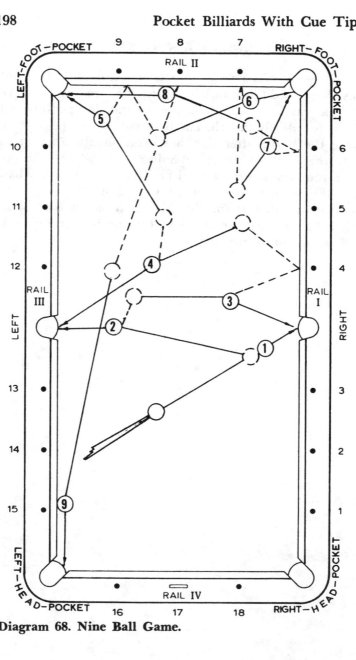

Diagram 68. Nine Ball Game.

Diagram 68—Nine Ball Game

Ball No.	How to Strike the Cue Ball
1	Center
2	6 o'clock, nip draw
3	9 o'clock
4	6 o'clock, nip draw
5	9 o'clock, soft
6	Center, medium
7	Center, soft
8	Center
9	Winning ball

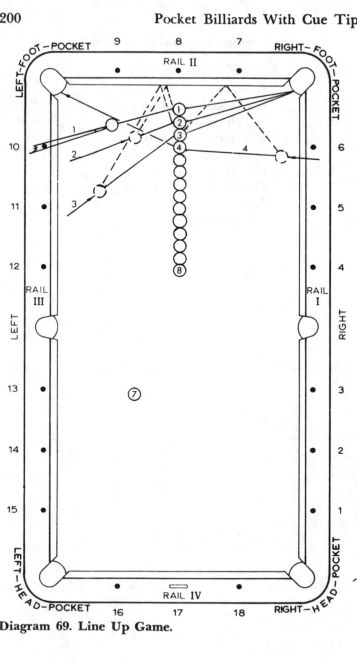

Diagram 69. Line Up Game.

Diagram 69—Line Up Game

In the game of Line Up there are usually many balls spotted along the foot-spot long string because after a player pockets all 15 balls, or until he misses, he is required to spot on the foot-spot long string all the balls he has pocketed. Therefore a player of this game should specialize and take advantage of his ability to play a lot of shots with the balls thus lined up. Here is where the draw, and follow techniques come in handy.

In shots 1 and 2 you can use the draw, striking the cue ball at 6 o'clock. For shot 3 you can still use the draw, but you may prefer to use a follow stroke in the hope that you can get the cue ball in a position where you can play ball 4 in the Left-Foot-Pocket and at the same time break up the string of balls. You sometimes get the opportunity of breaking up the balls by playing a ball in the side pocket (the 8-ball in this instance).

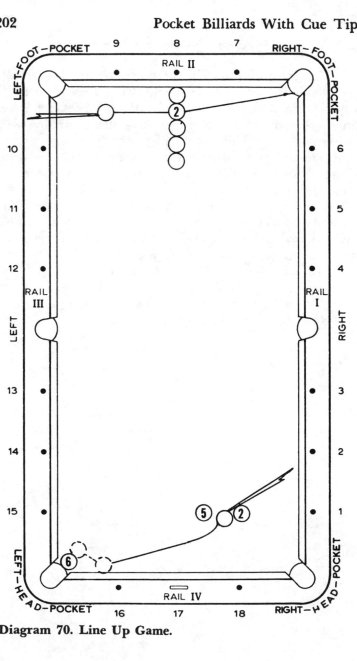

Diagram 70. Line Up Game.

Diagram 70—Line Up Game

The 2-ball can be pocketed in the Right-Foot-Pocket with a forced draw shot, striking the cue ball at 4 o'clock or 5 o'clock.

At the head end of the table the 6-ball can be pocketed by using a 30 percent massé shot. Elevate the handle of your cue about 30 percent, which should make the cue ball skirt around ball 5, then roll toward Rail IV and hit ball 6.

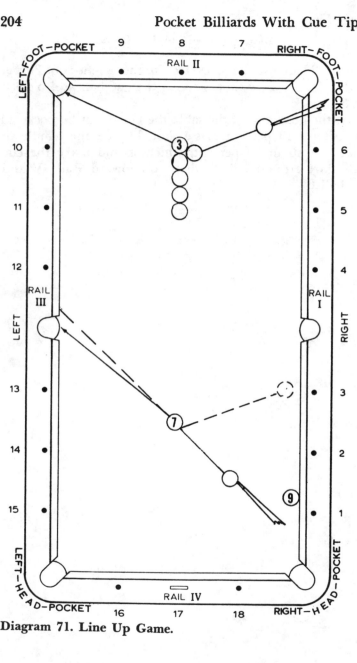

Diagram 71. Line Up Game.

Diagram 71—Line Up Game

The string of balls at the foot of the table is a common one in the Line Up game and presents the striker with an opportunity to break up the balls. To pocket ball 3 in the Left-Foot-Pocket simply strike the cue ball so as to give the correct angle cut on ball 3. In the event that the angle shot to the corner pocket is one that the player has doubt about successfully making, he should resort to a safety. Strike the cue ball delicately so that it will hit Rail I and then bounce back sufficiently to touch but not break up the string of balls.

At the head end of the table, ball 7 should be pocketed in the Left-Side-Pocket with a *straight-on* shot. But the cue ball must then be struck at 5 o'clock in order to throw the 7-ball slightly to the left and into the side pocket. The cue ball then draws back to Rail I where it will be in position to pocket ball 9.

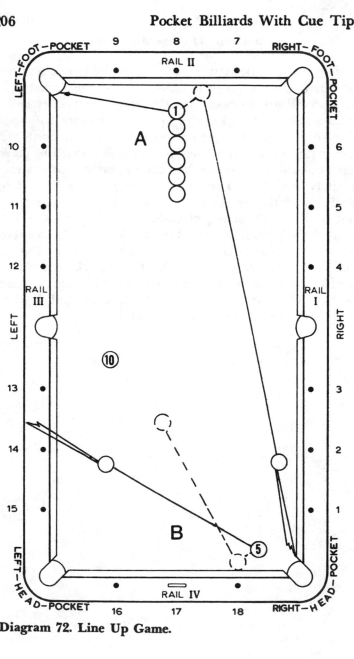

Diagram 72. Line Up Game.

Diagram 72—Line Up Game

Shot A is one that presents itself often in the Line Up game. It is really a very easy shot. All you have to do to pocket ball 1 in the Left-Foot-Pocket is to use left English and then hit the end rail *first*. This shot can be made when the ball to be pocketed is as far away from the end rail as 4½ inches, which is the width of two balls. (The English used is always in the direction in which the ball will be pocketed.)

Shot B requires a slight cut on the 5-ball. To get position on ball 10, strike the cue ball with slight draw effect at 4 o'clock or 5 o'clock.

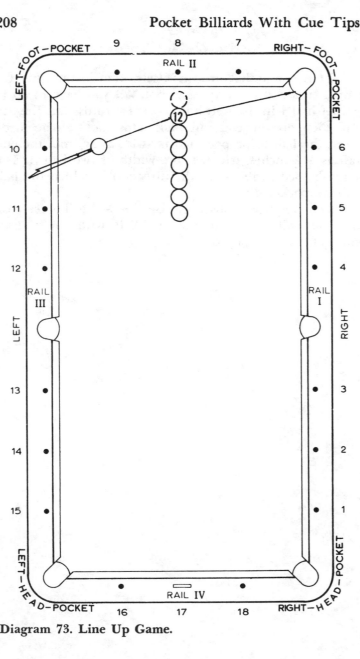

Diagram 73. Line Up Game.

Diagram 73—Line Up Game

Here is the perfect disaster shot. By playing ball 12 in the Right-Foot-Pocket with a normal stroke, you will often make your cue ball hit Rail II and then bounce back and rest right *behind* the string of balls. To prevent this from happening you must use either the draw or the follow technique, otherwise you are *Kaput,* finished, and your opponent takes over.

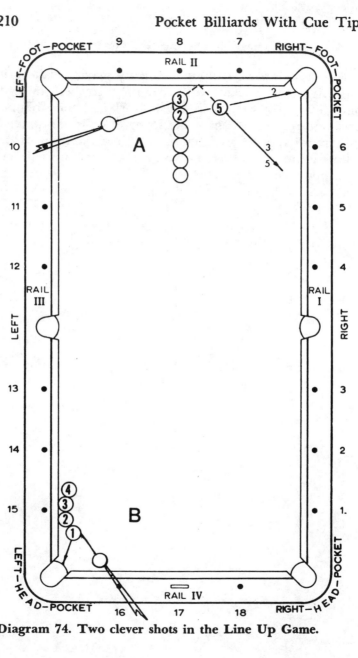

Diagram 74. Two clever shots in the Line Up Game.

Diagram 74—Two Clever Shots in Line Up

Shot A. Ball 2 can be pocketed in the Right-Foot-Pocket with a billiard (carom) shot on ball 3. What happens is this: ball 3 hits Rail II and then hits ball 5 so that both balls roll in the direction of the arrow. This clears a path for ball 2 to roll toward and into the Right-Foot-Pocket. Strike the cue ball at 2 o'clock.

Shot B. Strike the cue ball at 3 o'clock with a soft touch. The counterclockwise spin of the cue ball then imparts a clockwise spin to ball 1, keeping it away from Rail III. The weight of balls 2, 3, and 4 acts as a wall from which ball 1 bounces back sufficiently to enter the pocket.

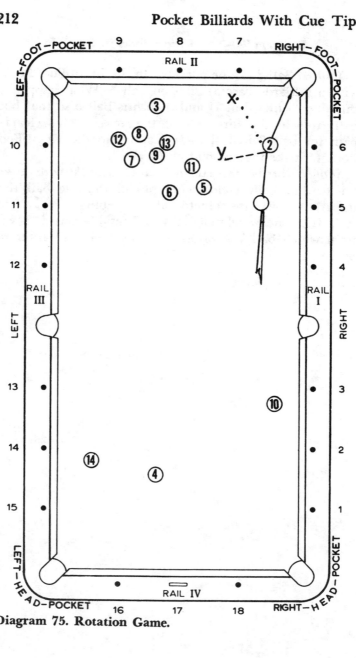

Diagram 75. Rotation Game.

Diagram 75—Rotation Game

Here, in shooting the 2-ball, one should play position on two balls ahead, the 3-ball and 4-ball. If one follows through to position X, one will be in a position to make the 3-ball but not able to then play position on the 4-ball, because in making the 3-ball from position X, the cue ball will be forced to plow into the cluster of balls near the rack area. Instead, in pocketing ball 2, one should strike the cue ball at 7 o'clock, executing a gentle draw to position Y. From Y one can pocket ball 3 and strike the cue ball at 5 o'clock, drawing it away from the bunch of balls to Rail II, then to Rail I, and up the table to ball 4.

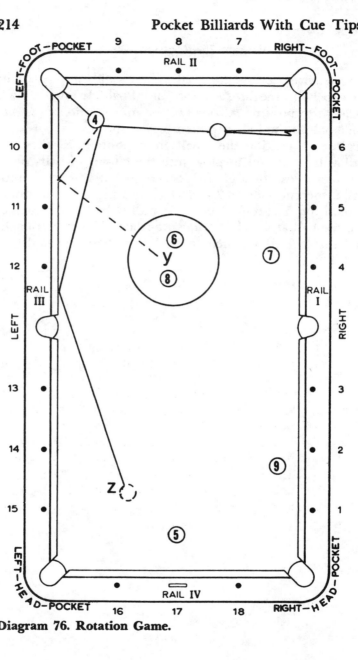

Diagram 76. Rotation Game.

Diagram 76—Rotation Game

To pocket ball 4 and play position on the 5-ball, one must avoid area Y. Therefore a simple draw at 6 o'clock should get the cue ball to the vicinity of Z. Use medium force!

Diagram 77—Rotation Game

Ball No.	How to Strike the Cue Ball
1	6 o'clock
2	Strike slightly above center with enough force to get position on ball 3 by banking across the table twice
3	6 o'clock, nip draw
4	7 o'clock, soft
5	Hit Rail II and the 5-ball simultaneously

Diagram 78—Miscellaneous

Shot A. This shot is appropriate for the game of One Pocket. Pocket ball 6, striking the cue ball at 9 o'clock to get position on ball 12.

Shot B. This is a side pocket, Kiss-Bank-Time shot. Strike the cue ball moderately at 11:00 or 11:30. Ball 4 moves toward the side pocket while the cue ball banks back from Rail I in time to pocket ball 4 in the Left-Side-Pocket. Here the timing—English used and force of your stroke—must be just right.

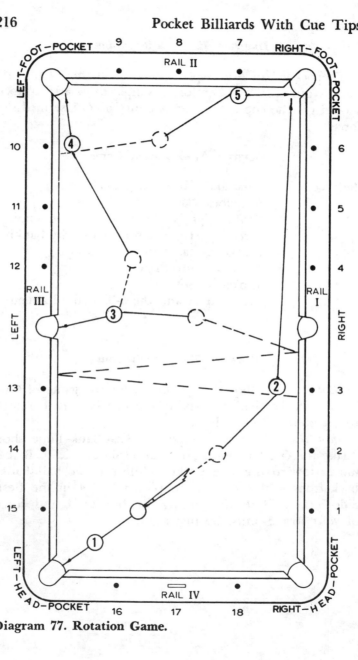

Diagram 77. Rotation Game.

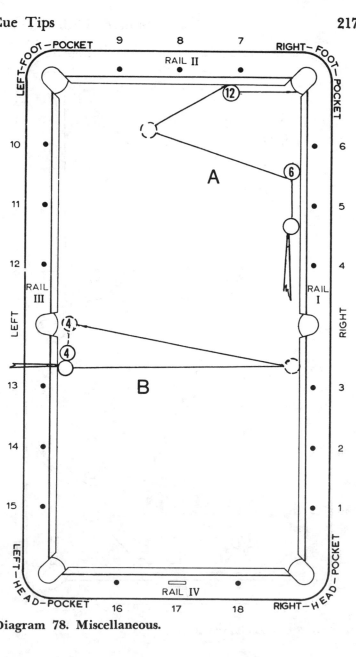

Diagram 78. Miscellaneous.

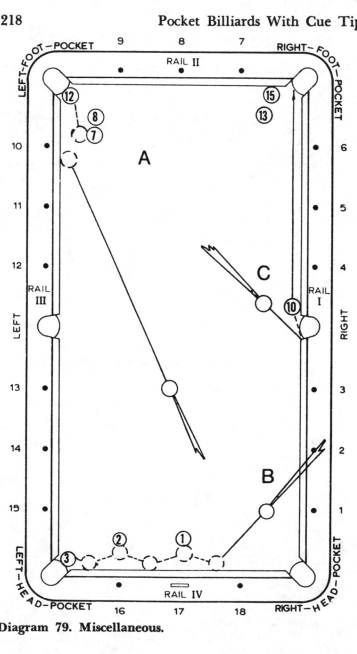

Diagram 79. Miscellaneous.

Diagram 79—Miscellaneous

Shot A. This is a single ticky shot. The cue ball hits Rail III, then ticks ball 7, and caroms off that ball to pocket ball 12.

Shot B. This is a double ticky shot since the cue ball caroms off two object balls (1 and 2) before it hits the ball to be pocketed.

Shot C. A playable shot is the 10-ball. Your best bet to pocket it is to have your cue ball hit the corner of the side pocket cushion. Even though the 10-ball does not roll directly toward the pocket, it may still go in by kissing off either ball 13 or ball 15.

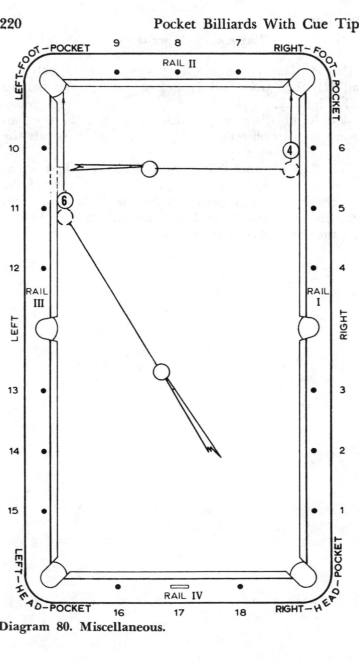

Diagram 80. Miscellaneous.

Diagram 80—Miscellaneous

To pocket ball 6 use a center medium stroke and aim the cue ball to hit the cushion and object ball *simultaneously.*

To pocket ball 4 requires a very thin cut. Aim the cue ball to hit the cushion slightly *behind* ball 4 and, in this shot, apply left English (9 o'clock), which will have the effect of nursing ball 4 to hug the cushion on its way to the pocket.

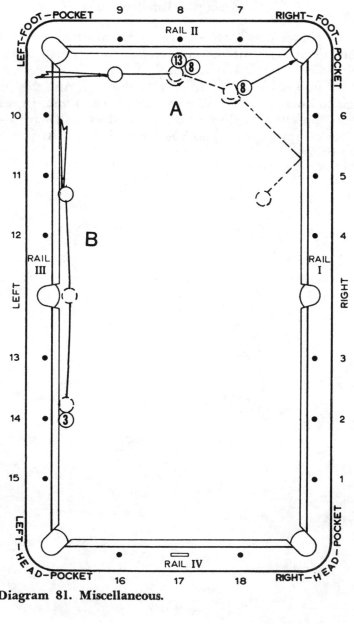

Diagram 81. Miscellaneous.

Diagram 81—Miscellaneous

Shot A. Here are two balls (13 and 8) lying in such a position that the average player would immediately say there was nothing that could be done with them. Yet, ball 8 can be pocketed in the Right-Foot-Pocket. If you strike the cue ball softly at 1 or 2 o'clock and hit the 13-ball very thinly, ball 13 bounces away from the cushion and moves ball 8 in the direction of spot 6; but before ball 8 rolls hardly any distance, the cue ball catches up with it and, because of the right English, throws ball 8 to the left and into the corner pocket.

Shot B. This is not a massé shot. You simply strike the cue ball moderately at 5 o'clock, which veers the cue ball sufficiently away from the cushion to insure that it will not hit the long angle of the side pocket. It then rolls back toward the cushion and pockets ball 3 in the Left-Head-Pocket. The reason for striking the cue ball at 5 o'clock is not only to keep it from hitting the corner of the side pocket but also to hold it from following ball 3 too far and scratching.

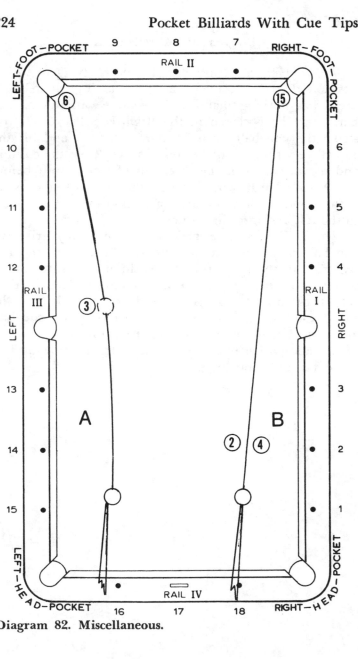

Diagram 82. Miscellaneous.

Diagram 82—Miscellaneous

Shot A shows how you can skirt around an obstructive object ball by using the massé technique. In this shot you elevate the cue about 30 percent and strike the cue ball moderately hard on its left side.

Shot B shows a jump shot. Here the cue ball is an ideal distance, about eight inches, away from the balls to be jumped over (2 and 4). Elevate your cue about 30 percent and strike hard downward on the cue ball. This makes the cue ball bounce up slightly above the horizontal axis of the two object balls where there is more room for it to pass. (See photograph in Chapter 12.) Jump shots are extremely precarious for beginners as they might rip up the cloth in attempting them.

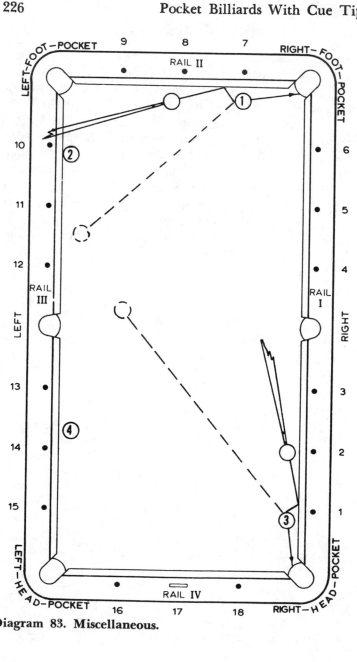

Diagram 83. Miscellaneous.

Diagram 83—Miscellaneous

This diagram shows two Cue-Ball-Cushion-First draw shots: one to pocket ball 1 and get position on ball 2; the other to pocket ball 3 and get position on ball 4. Strike the cue ball at 6 o'clock and have it hit the cushion first.

Diagram 84—Miscellaneous

Shot A. The cue ball is at the rail making it necessary to use a follow shot. This long shot is not an easy one. To get position on ball 6 use a soft stroke and be sure the cue ball hits the 5-ball and the cushion at *the same time.*

Shot B. You can make this shot by striking the cue ball very hard at 11 o'clock giving it a good spin resulting in a "kissing" action between the cue ball and object ball. The cue ball (too quick for the eye to see) actually hits the 7-ball twice. Perhaps a better way of stating this is that the 7-ball for lack of anywhere else to go is forced into the pocket. Here the 7-ball must be frozen to the rail and hanging-up in the pocket, and the cue ball must hit it so as not to drive it in the pocket but force it in. After pocketing the 7-ball the cue ball hits Rail IV, bounces back only a short distance and because of its powerful overspin it then moves back toward Rail IV where you will have position on ball 8.

Diagram 85—Miscellaneous

Here is a shot that can be made in three different ways to give you position on ball 2:

  (a) 7 o'clock, forced draw

  (b) 9 o'clock, soft. Hit the 1-ball slightly to the right of center.

  (c) 2 o'clock, soft, which will deflect the cue ball from Rail I to position (c).

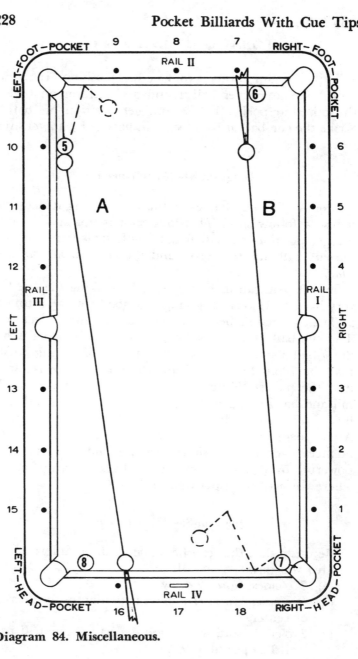

Diagram 84. Miscellaneous.

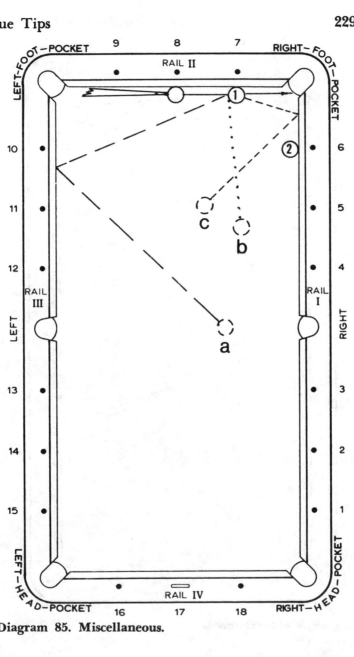

Diagram 85. Miscellaneous.

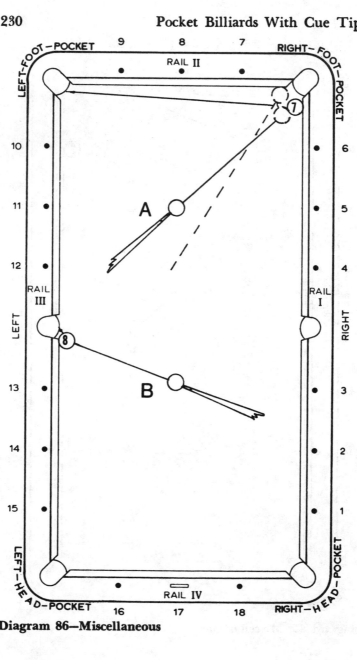

Diagram 86—Miscellaneous

Diagram 86—Miscellaneous

Shot A. In the One Pocket game where yours is the Left-Foot-Pocket and the only playable shot is the 7-ball, you can bank this ball into your pocket by a *hard* follow stroke, hitting the 7-ball at 3/4 left. While the 7-ball is being pressed to the cushion the cue ball has a chance to hit the end rail and bounce back in time so as to allow the 7-ball to bank to the Left-Foot-Pocket.

Shot B. To pocket ball 8 in the side pocket strike the cue ball hard at 12 o'clock and hit ball 8 at its dead center.

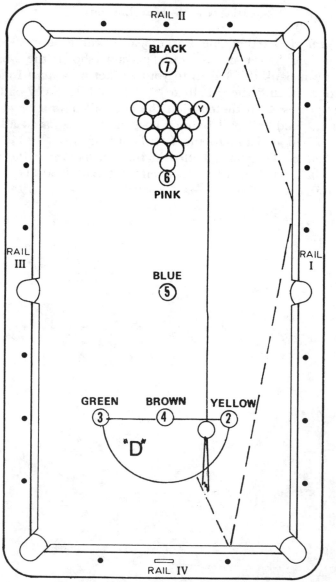

Diagram 87. American Snooker Game.

Diagram 87—American Snooker Game

Break shot. This should always be a safe shot. The cue ball is placed anywhere within the "D" (half circle at the head of the table), preferably as shown. Then the cue ball should be struck with only sufficient force when glancing off the red object ball Y to come back off the foot rail to the head of the table in a safe position, with even the possibility of snookering your opponent by leaving the cue ball behind either the 2, 3, or 4 balls. The professionals use a more sophisticated break shot.

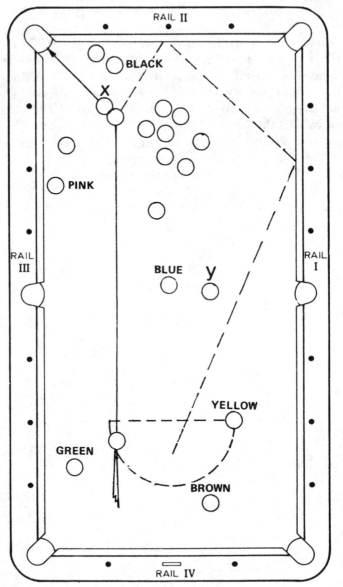

Diagram 88. American Snooker Game.

Diagram 88—American Snooker Game

Although the easiest shot on the red balls is ball Y, the wiser shot is to try to pocket red ball X as indicated for two reasons: *First,* it is a safer shot. If you shoot ball Y and miss your cue ball will run into the cluster of red balls and undoubtedly give your opponent an easy shot, whereas if you miss ball X, you should at least be able to get the cue ball back up the head part of the table and in a fairly safe position, and *secondly,* it is a better position-play shot. If one is successful in pocketing red ball Y in the side pocket the chances are you will not have a very good shot on a required numbered ball, especially since the black ball is in bad position to be made, whereas if one is successful in pocketing ball X the chances are much better that he will have fairly good position on either the yellow, green or brown balls.

Glossary of Pocket Billiard Terms

AMERICAN SNOOKER: *See* SNOOKER.

ANGLE: The relationship of the cue ball to its first or second object ball

ANGLED (SNOOKERED): When the corner of a pocket or an obstructing ball prevents a player shooting the cue ball in a direct line at his object ball

ANGLES: *Long Angle* is the bend or return of a pocket farthest away from you (the side of the pocket that greets you) when pocketing a ball from a slanting position.
Short Angle is the side of the same pocket nearest you.
See also NARROW ANGLE, WIDE ANGLE.

BALANCE POINT: The point of balance of the cue

BALL IN HAND: *See* CUE BALL IN HAND.

BALL OFF THE TABLE: When a ball jumps off the bed of the table

BALL-ON: A ball is on when a player can shoot at it in a straight line or when it can be driven into a called pocket on a combination or carom shot.

BALLS HIT SIMULTANEOUSLY: It is permissible to hit balls simultaneously in call-shot pocket billiards, provided the player calls both ball and pocket.

BALLS TOUCHING: *See* FROZEN.

BANK SHOT: When a player drives an object ball against a cushion before pocketing it

BED OF TABLE: The base of the table

BEHIND THE HEAD STRING: The table area at the head of the table between Spots 2 and 14 and between the Head String and Rail IV

BREAK: The opening shot of the game

BREAKER: The player who breaks the rack of balls

BRIDGE: The formation of the player's hand in holding and guiding the tip end of the cue shaft in stroking; it is also a cue-like stick (MECHANICAL BRIDGE or V BRIDGE) with a notched plate at the tip end, which a player may use as an aid in making long shots difficult to reach.

BUMPER: The rubber bottom of the cue used for resting the cue on the floor when it is not in use

CALLED BALL: The ball that a player announces he intends to pocket

CALLED POCKET: The pocket into which a player intends to drop a called ball

CAROM: *See* KISS.

CARRYING CASE: A hard or soft case for carrying the cue

CLOCK DIAL METHOD: A method employed by which a player strikes (contacts) the cue ball at points corresponding to the dial of a clock

COMBINATION SHOT: A shot in which the player sets in motion one or more balls between the cue ball and object ball so that the last one hits the called ball

CONTACT POINT: A point at which the cue ball and object ball meet when hitting each other; this applies also between one or more object balls.

CONTINUOUS 14.1: *See* FOURTEEN-ONE CONTINUOUS.

COUNTING STRING: The string above the playing table on which to tally your score

CUE BALL: The ball a player shoots with or strikes with the cue

CUE BALL ANGLED: *See* ANGLED.

CUE BALL IN HAND: A player has a cue ball in hand when,

as the result of a foul or error on the part of his opponent, or as the result of some other governing situation, he puts the ball in play at a point of his choice behind the head string

CUEING-BEHIND-BACK: Unorthodox style of shooting with the cue behind one's back

CUEING THE BALL: Striking, stroking, or addressing the cue ball with the tip of the cue

CUSHION: The cloth covered resilient ridge that borders the inside of the four rails

CUT: To hit an object ball less than full at the center, causing the ball to deflect at an angle

DEAD BALL: The cue ball becomes a dead ball when it is struck dead center giving it no English (spin or twist) and hits an object ball perfectly straight-on.

DEAD BALL SHOT: A shot executed to produce a dead ball

DEAD-IN SHOT: A straight-in shot. See also BALL-ON.

DIAMONDS: See SPOTS

DOWN THE TABLE: Refers to the foot end of the table where the balls are racked

DRAW: Cueing the cue ball below center, causing it to reverse its original forward roll so that it draws back from the object ball it has hit
Opposite of FOLLOW

DROP IT IN: To pocket a ball, lay it up in the pocket, make it

EIGHT BALL: A game in which one player pockets balls numbered 1 to 7 and his opponent pockets balls 9 to 15; the 8-ball is pocketed last
(See Chapter 8, Various Pocket Billiard Games.)

ENGLISH: The result of striking the cue ball off its dead center, causing it to twist or spin

FANCY SHOT: A shot that requires unusual skill

FEATHERING: Hitting the object ball very thinly

FEEL OF A CUE: The feeling of a cue in your hands; its comfortableness

FERRULE: The one-inch segment of the cue below its tip, usually made of buckhorn

FOLLOW: Cueing the cue ball above center, causing it to follow in the same general direction after hitting the object ball; opposite of DRAW

FOLLOW-THROUGH: The follow movement of the cue, after contact with the cue ball, through the area occupied by the cue ball before it was struck by the cue; an important fundamental in striking the cue ball

FOOT OF TABLE: The end of the table where the balls are racked

FOOT SPOT: The spot at the foot of the table where the balls are racked at the start of pocket billiard games

FORCE: The amount of force applied in striking the cue ball

FORCE DRAW: Forcing the cue ball "through" the object ball before the cue ball begins to draw back so as to increase the drawing effect on the cue ball

FORCE FOLLOW: Forcing the cue ball "through" the object ball or driving the cue ball a more-than-usual distance after it hits the object ball

FOUL: An infraction of game rules

FOUL STROKE: An infraction of game rules as the result of a player's stroke, such as pushing the cue ball or two separate contacts of the cue tip on the cue ball

FOURTEEN-ONE-CONTINUOUS: A call-shot game; after 14 balls are pocketed they are racked without a ball being put on the foot spot. Player then pockets the 15th ball from the position where it rests on the table. In doing so he tries to have the cue ball break up the newly racked 14 balls. (*See* Chapter 8, Various Pocket Billiard Games.)

FROZEN: Two or more balls touching each other; also a ball resting against a cushion is said to be frozen

FULCRUM POINT: The point of balance of the cue

FULL BALL: Contact of the cue ball with an object ball at

its precise center as opposed to a ball that is cut ¾, ½, ¼, etc

GAME: Particular name of a game being played; also, a player claims GAME when he wins.

GLIDE SHOT: Drawing the cue ball with English; used in short distance shots

GRIP: Player's hold on the handle of the cue

GULLIES: Runways at the sides of the table that carry balls, as they are pocketed, to one or more compartments on the outside of and below the foot rail

HANDLE OF CUE: The lower, heavy half of the cue that the player grips when addressing the cue ball

HEAD OF TABLE: The short rail (Rail IV) that bears the manufacturer's name plate

HEAD STRING: A line that runs from Spot 2 on the right side of the table to Spot 14 on the left side of the table; the area between the head string and the head of the table is where you place the cue ball in starting most games of pocket billiards.

HIGH RUN: The largest consecutive points scored by a player in one inning of a game

HIT: The cue ball HITS the object ball; the object balls HIT each other and HIT the cushions. (The cue STRIKES the cue ball.)

HOLD: Any action applied to hold the cue ball back from the course it would normally take, such as in stop shots, draw shots, near-stop shots and reverse English

HUG THE RAIL: A ball that stays close to a rail; action on the cue ball can make it roll along or bounce several times against the rail

HUSTLER: Reference to one who generally travels from community to community gambling at the sport in an effort to make a living

IMAGINARY POINT: If the object ball is cut less than one-half you must aim at an imaginary point beyond the object ball; the thinner your cut, the farther away will be this imaginary point. (*See* Diagram 12, Chapter 13.)

INNING: A turn at the table that is terminated when the player misses

IN STROKE: A player is IN STROKE when he is performing well with a perfect, even, rhythmic stroke of the cue.

JOINT OF CUE: The middle part of the cue for coupling the two halves of the cue together

JUMP SHOT: A MASSÉ shot executed with cue handle elevated about 30 percent

JUMPED BALL: A ball that jumps off the bed of the table

KISS: A KISS means a CAROM. The cue ball may KISS (deflect) from one object ball to another or more object balls. An object ball may KISS one or more object balls

LAG: To determine which player starts a game; each shoots the cue ball from behind the head string to the foot rail from which it bounces back to the head rail. The player whose ball rests closest to the head rail has the option to shoot first

LEAVE: The position in which the balls are left after a shot is played; hence the phrases: being left with a good LEAVE or a bad LEAVE

LIE OF BALL OR BALLS: The position of a ball where it lies after rolling and coming to rest (This word is used more by golfers than by billiard players.)

LINE UP: The method of spotting the object balls in the game of LINE UP pocket billiards

LINE UP GAME: A call-shot game; players are required to call the ball and the pocket into which it is to be dropped. (*See* Chapter 8, Various Pocket Billiard Games.)

LIVE BALL: A ball that is in play under the rules of a game; also, the cue ball when its action is alive as opposed to a DEAD BALL

LONG: In pocket billiards a ball rolls LONG when it comes

off a cushion at a wide angle.

LONG ANGLE OF POCKET: The corner of a pocket farthest away from you (the one that greets you) as you are pocketing a ball from a slanting angle

LONG STRING: An imaginary line (drawn for tournament playing) from the foot spot to the center of the foot rail, on which balls are spotted

MAKE IT: To pocket a ball, drop it in, lay it up in the pocket

MASSÉ: Extreme application of ENGLISH

MECHANICAL BRIDGE: *See* BRIDGE.

MISCUE: Faulty stroking; a stroke in which the cue tip slips from the cue ball due to a defective tip, improper chalking of the cue tip, or excessive application of English

MISS: Failure of a player to successfully pocket his called shot, ending his inning

NARROW ANGLE: When the cue ball is struck with reverse English in order to impart hold action, which also narrows its angle

NATURAL: A simple shot

NINE BALL: A game played with a cue ball and nine balls numbered one through nine; the object of the game is to legally pocket the 9-ball. This is not a call-shot game, as opposed to 14.1 CONTINUOUS and LINE UP games

NIP DRAW STROKE: A short light stroke, executed delicately with wrist action

ON BALL: *See* BALL ON

ONE POCKET: A game played with a cue ball and 15 numbered balls; prior to the opening shot one pocket at the foot of the table is selected by the winner of the lag as the pocket he will use. The other person or side will then use only the other pocket at the foot of the table. First player to legally pocket eight balls in the pocket assigned him shall be declared winner of the game

PACK: A cluster of balls

PINCH DRAW SHOT: When (1) the cue ball lies very close to an object ball and you wish to draw, it is necessary to employ a quick, jerky (PINCH) stroke to avoid having the cue ball come back into the cue, which must be pulled away or (2) when an object ball is close behind your cue ball and you wish to draw, it is necessary to employ both an abbreviated (PINCH) BRIDGE and DRAW in order to avoid having the cue ball come back into the cue and object ball behind it. *See* NIP DRAW SHOT

PIQUET SHOT: A draw shot that reverses the direction of the cue ball without its having hit an object ball; a trick shot

POCKET A BALL: To drop it in, lay it up in the pocket, make it

POCKET BILLIARDS: *The Official Rule Book* lists 18 different kinds of pocket billiard games.

POINT OF AIM: The point to which you direct the cue ball in order to have it meet the object ball at the CONTACT POINT you have predetermined *See also* IMAGINARY POINT

POSITION PLAYING: Controlling the distance the cue ball has to roll so that you can position it in a favorable spot for your next shot

PRONGS: The crown or the four dark points immediately above the cue handle wrapping

PUSH SHOT: Shoving or pushing the cue ball with the tip of the cue, or two contacts of the cue tip on the cue ball; if the stroke is made with one continuous motion it may be allowed, provided there is prior agreement between the players. In tournament playing, the referee is the sole judge of push shot legality

PYRAMID: The placement of object balls in a triangle on the foot spot to start a game (Racking the balls)

RACK: The wooden triangle used to pyramid balls on the foot spot for the opening shot in pocket billiard games; it also describes the arrangement of the object balls after the triangle is removed

RAIL: The two long and two short panels above the table bed from which the cushions slope; the long RAIL to the right of the head of the table is Rail I, that at the foot of the table is Rail II, that at the left of the head of the table is Rail III, and that at the head of the table that bears the manufacturer's name is Rail IV.

REVERSE: ENGLISH applied to put HOLD on the ball; a spin that makes the cue ball bounce off a cushion at a more obtuse angle and at a slower speed than a ball to which no ENGLISH has been imparted or a ball to which natural (RUNNING) ENGLISH has been imparted

ROTATION: A non-call-shot game; however, players are required to shoot at and pocket balls in their numerical order. (See Chapter 8, Various Pocket Billiard Games.)

RUN: A series of consecutive scores in one inning

RUNNING ENGLISH: Slight FOLLOW and ENGLISH favoring the cue ball's progress, right or left in the direction of the shot, giving the ball a natural run

SAFETY: A defensive maneuver to which a player can resort when confronted with a difficult shot; he sacrifices an opportunity to score and ends his inning in an attempt to leave his opponent with a difficult shot.

SCORE STRING: The string above the playing table on which to tally your score.

SCRATCH: The cue ball going into a pocket, which means forfeiture of one point in most of the games and the end of your inning

SET UP: An easy shot

SHAFT: The upper, slender half of the cue

SHOOTER: The player who shoots or strikes the cue ball

SHORT: In pocket billiards a ball rolls SHORT when it comes off a cushion at a narrow angle

SHORT ANGLE OF POCKET: The corner of a pocket nearest you when pocketing a ball from a slanting angle

SLIDE SHOT: Drawing the cue ball delicately with or without English; used in short distance shots

SNOOKER: A game played with 21 object balls and cue ball on a 5' x 10' or a 6' x 12' table; the game is also played on 4' x 8' and 4½' x 9' tables. Balls and pockets are smaller than those of a regular pocket billiard table

SNOOKERED: *See* ANGLED

SPEED CONTROL: The amount of force applied to the cue ball

SPLITTING THE POCKET: When an object ball is perfectly pocketed so that it enters at the exact center of the pocket

SPOT BALL: A ball that is placed at the foot, center, or head spot to conform with the game's rules

SPOT SHOT: When a player shoots at a ball that has been placed on a spot

SPOTS: The spots (also called diamonds) on the rails of a pocket billiard table; the numbers, 1 to 18, start to the right of the Right-Head-Pocket, going toward the right foot end of the table in counterclockwise fashion. (*See* Diagram 2.)

SPOTTING: The placement or replacement of the balls on the table as required by the rules of the game; also a term used when a player allows another player a head start of score counts (points)

SQUEEZE SHOT: When either (1) the cue ball has to squeeze by on either side of an object ball in order to reach and pocket another object ball or (2) when a called ball has to squeeze by on either side of another object ball on its way to a called pocket (*See* Diagram 65.)

STANCE: The position of the player when addressing himself to the cue ball

STICK: A cue, a cueist, a player; an expert is sometimes referred to as a top stick

STOP SHOT: When the cue ball is struck dead center with full impact and stops rolling upon hitting an object ball or displacing it

STRAIGHT-IN: A shot where the cue ball, object ball, and pocket are in a straight line

STRAIGHT-ON: Having the cue ball hit the center of the object ball

STRIKE: Your cue STRIKES the cue ball. (The cue ball HITS an object ball. Also the object balls HIT each other and HIT the cushions.)

STRIKER: The player who STRIKES or shoots the cue ball

STRING: The string above the table for each player to keep track of his scored points

STROKE: The swinging motion of the cue in the player's hands

THROW SHOT: Diverting an object ball from its natural direction; for instance when two object balls, or the cue ball and an object ball, are frozen to or separated from each other by not more than one-quarter inch

TIP OF CUE: The leather cap attached to the tip end of the cue's shaft

TOP STICK: An expert player

TRIANGLE: The wooden rack for setting up the balls on the foot spot

TRICK SHOT: An out-of-the-ordinary shot used in exhibition playing

TRIGGERING THE CUE BALL: To let go with your stroke on the cue ball like a sharpshooter lets go when he pulls on the gun's trigger

UP THE TABLE: Refers to the head end of the table where you stand when starting a game; the table manufacturer's name is shown here

WIDE ANGLE: When stroking the cue ball with slight follow and English that accelerates the rolling action of the cue ball and widens its angle

WING SHOT: *(used in exhibitions)*: An object ball is rolled on the table and pocketed while it is still in motion

WRAPPING OF CUE: The wrapping on the handle of the cue

Bibliography

Books

Billiard Congress of America. *Billiards—Knowing and Playing Pocket and 3-Cushion*. Chicago, 1968.

Billiard Congress of America. *Official Rule and Record Book.* Chicago, 1968.

Billiard proprietors and players. *First Five Years of Chalk Up.* A compilation of newsletters for Billiard and Recreation Management, (126 pages.) 1966.

Brothe, Clint. Billiard Diamonds.

Brunswick-Balke-Collender Co., ed. *Modern Billiards*. New York: Brunswick-Balke-Collender Co., 1891.

———. *One Hundred Years of Recreation*. Chicago: Brunswick-Balke-Collender Co., 1945.

Burrows Corporation. *How to Play Pool (pamphlet)*. Portland, Maine.

Caras, Jimmie. *Trick and Fancy Shots in Pocket Billiards.* Springfield, Pennsylvania, 1948.

Cottingham, Jr., Clive. *The Game of Billiards.* Philadelphia: J. B. Lippincott Co., 1964.

Daly, Maurice. *Daly's Billiard Book.* Chicago, 1916.

Fensch, Thomas. *The Lions and the Lambs.* South Brunswick and New York: A. S. Barnes and Company, 1970.

Garnier, Albert. *Garnier's Practice Shots.* New York, 1880.

———. *Scientific Billiards.* New York, 1880.

Henning, E. P. *The Hoosier Pocket Billiard Champion.* Indianapolis, 1913.

Herrmann, Fred. *Fun on the Pool Table.* New York, 1902.

Hoppe, Willie. *Billiards As It Should be Played.* Chicago: The Reilly and Lee Co., 1941. (Author's note: While this excellent book is primarily on billiards, much of the first 40 pages is also applicable to *pocket* billiards.)

———. *Thirty Years of Billiards.* New York, 1925.

Lassiter, Luther. *Billiards for Everyone*. New York: Grosset.

———. *The Modern Guide to Pocket Billiards*. New York: Fleet Publishing Co., 1964.

McCleery, Professor J. F. B. *The McCleery Method of Billiard Playing*. San Francisco, 1890.

Minnesota Fats, with Tom Fox. *The Bank Shot and Other Great Robberies*. Cleveland: The World Publishing Co., 1966.

Mosconi, Willie. *Willie Mosconi on Pocket Billiards*. New York: Crown Publishers, Inc., 1948.

———. *Winning Pocket Billiards*. New York: Crown Publishers, Inc., 1965.

Phelan, Michael. *Billiards Without a Master*. New York, 1850.

———. *The Game of Billiards*. New York, 1858, 1866.

Storer, C. A. *The Complete Fundamentals of Billiards*. Authorized by National Billiard Association of America, 1934.

Sullivan, George and Crane, Irving. *The Young Sportsman's Guide to Pocket Billiards*. New York: Thomas Nelson & Sons, 1964.

Author's note: Not listed but available are over 125 books on billiards, published in England and other countries.

Magazines and Newspapers

Billiard Congress of America. *Bulletin*. 20 North Wacker Drive, Chicago, Illinois 60606. (Issued occasionally)

Luby, Mort, Jr., editor and publisher. *The National Bowlers Journal and Billiard Revue*. 506 South Wabash Avenue, Chicago, Illinois 60605. (Monthly)

Newby, Earl, editor and publisher. *The National Billiard News*. 1035 Chestnut Street, Philadelphia, Pa. 19107. (Monthly)

Wise, Jimmy. *Phonograph Record "Pocket Billiards"* 33
    Long Play Record. 794 Johnston Street, Half Moon
    Bay, Ca. 94019.

The Billiard Archives, 154 La Verne Avenue, Long
Beach, California 90803, carry a stock of current and old
books on all games of billiards. They have rare copies of
magazines and newspapers, unusual photographs, prints,
and miscellaneous items, all having to do with billiards.
A partial list follows:
Books et cetera
Billiard Association and Control Council. *Billiards As-
    sociation and Control Council Handbook.* Fully
    illustrated containing the rules and various games
    and new and interesting information about billiards
    and snooker. London.
Burroughs and Watts. *Billiards Simplified or How to
    Make Breaks.* London: Burroughs & Watts. 1884,
    1889.
Clifford, W. G. *How to Play and Win at Snooker.* Lon-
    don: Adam and Charles Black.
Collender, H. W., ed. *The Billiard Cue.* (A four-page
    newspaper.) New York, February 1874.
Davis, Joe. *How I Play Snooker.* London: Country Life,
    Ltd., 1949.
———. *Improve Your Snooker.* London: Methuen & Co.,
    Ltd., 1946.
Holt, Richard. *Billiards and Snooker.* (A volume in the
    famous *Teach Yourself Books.*) London: The Uni-
    versities Press, Ltd. 1957.
———. *Billiards and Snooker: Know the Game.* Yorkshire:
    Educational Productions, Ltd., 1958.
Hoppe, Willie. *Physical Culture Magazine.* (Contains
    three-page article and pictures on Willie Hoppe.)
    New York, July 1921.
Lindrum, Horace. *Billiards and Snooker for Amateurs.*
    London, 1962.

Newman, Stanley. *How to Play Snooker.* London, 1948.

White, E., Esq. *Practical Treatise on the Game of Billiards.* London. W. Bulmer & Company, 1807. Referred to as the first book published on billiards. 1807, 1818.

The World of Billiards. Three large volumes of this unusual English billiard magazine covering 1901, 1902, and 1903.

Prints

Braque, Georges. *Le Billard.* (From Braque's abstract painting of a billiard table; original in Louvre, Paris) 17" x 24", full color ($3.00).

French Soldier at Billiard Table. (In nineteenth-century costume) color lithograph, 11" x 8" plus margins ($20.00).

Ladies' Battle, A. (Young women in costume of 1880s playing at billiard table) 17" x 22", black and white ($6.00).

Man in Tuxedo at Billiard Table. Color lithograph, 12½" x 7½" plus margins ($20.00).

Van Gogh, Vincent. *Cafe at Night in Arles.* (From original by famed artist Van Gogh who painted cafe and billiard table in 1880s) 17½" x 24", full color ($12.00).

Women and Men at Billiard Table. (Scene in France in early 1880s) color lithograph, 9" x 12" plus margins ($65.00).

Photographs

Peter Sellers and Curved Cue. (From *A Shot in the Dark*) 8" x 10" ($5.00).

Still photos of action billiard scenes from the movie *The Hustler* starring Jackie Gleason and Paul Newman. 8" x 10" each ($6.90 for set of 10).

W. C. Fields and Famous Crooked Cue. 8" x 10" ($5.00).

Willie Hoppe, 1906 and 1909. (Two photos) Hoppe shown making shot with giant tournament medal, approximately 11" x 16" plus margins ($25.00).

Index

Index

Determination, 154
Diagram of the pocket billiard table, 47
Diagrams 42 to 88, with cue tips, 153–235
Draw shot, 36, 74–76, 111, 112, 131–137
    bridge for, 36
    draw shot exercise, 131–137
    exercise for corner and side pockets, 111, 112
    where to strike the cue ball, 74–76

Eight Ball game, 59–61
English (spinning or twisting of ball), 74, 79, 87–91, 102, 123–126
    a few words in general about its use, 87–91, 102, 123–126
    four basic types of, 74
    reverse English retards the speed of the cue ball, 102
    running English accelerates the speed of the cue ball, 102
    stroking hard closes the angle, 125, 126
    stroking gently opens the angle, 125, 126
    unintentional use of, 88, 89, 129
    use of, helpful on a thin shot, 79
    use of, in making bank shots, 123–126
    use of, on combination shots, 127–130
    use only when it is absolutely necessary, 89, 90
    where the tip of the cue strikes the cue ball is very important, 87
Exercise of body, 50
Exercises in pocket billiards, 92–96, 108–112, 119–127, 131–137
    center-ball, draw, follow, stop and near-stop, 131–137
    corner and side pocket draw shots, 111, 112

how to execute a true stop shot, 133, 136
long shots to the corner pocket, 108–110
natural or plain bank shots, 119–123
three interesting shots, 92–96
use of English on bank shots, 123–125
Experience necessary to improve your playing, 85, 153
    in aiming shot, 85
    in controlling the cue ball, 153
Eyes, alignment of, 43, 44

"Feel" in aiming shot, 85
"Feel" of the cue, 52
Fields, W. C., 250
Follow shot, 37, 38, 74–76, 133, 135
    bridge for, 37, 38
    exercise in, 133, 135
    where to strike the cue ball, 74–76
Follow-through stroke, 43–45
Force applied to the cue ball, 74, 98–104
Forced draw shot, 133
Fourteen-One Continuous game, 57, 58
Fractions method used in cutting the object ball, 81–84
Froeschle, Robert E., 50, 148
Frozen ball (use English when banking a ball that is frozen to the rail in order to avoid a collision between the object and cue balls), 120, 121
Fujima, Kazuo, 147
Full-ball shot, 78–84

Games, pocket billiard, 54–64
Glance, last, before shooting, 72, 73
Gleason, Jackie, photo of action billiard scene for sale, 250
Glossary of pocket billiard terms, 236–246
Gorecki, Jacquelyn, 27
Greenleaf, Ralph, 21, 22

A PERSONAL WORD FROM MELVIN POWERS, PUBLISHER, WILSHIRE BOOK COMPANY

My goal is to publish interesting, informative, and inspirational books. You can help me to accomplish this by sending me your answers to the following questions:

Did you enjoy reading this book? Why?

What ideas in the book impressed you most? Have you applied them to your daily life? How?

Is there a chapter that could serve as a theme for an entire book? Explain.

Would you like to read similar books? What additional information would you like them to contain?

If you have an idea for a book, I would welcome discussing it with you. If you have a manuscript in progress, write or call me concerning possible publication.

Melvin Powers
12015 Sherman Road
North Hollywood, California 91605

(818) 765-8579

MELVIN POWERS SELF-IMPROVEMENT LIBRARY

ASTROLOGY

____ ASTROLOGY—HOW TO CHART YOUR HOROSCOPE Max Heindel 7.00
____ ASTROLOGY AND SEXUAL ANALYSIS Morris C. Goodman 10.00
____ ASTROLOGY AND YOU Carroll Righter 5.00
____ ASTROLOGY MADE EASY Astarte 7.00
____ ASTROLOGY, ROMANCE, YOU AND THE STARS Anthony Norvell 10.00
____ MY WORLD OF ASTROLOGY Sydney Omarr 10.00
____ THOUGHT DIAL Sydney Omarr 7.00
____ WHAT THE STARS REVEAL ABOUT THE MEN IN YOUR LIFE Thelma White 3.00

BRIDGE

____ BRIDGE BIDDING MADE EASY Edwin B. Kantar 15.00
____ BRIDGE CONVENTIONS Edwin B. Kantar 10.00
____ COMPETITIVE BIDDING IN MODERN BRIDGE Edgar Kaplan 7.00
____ DEFENSIVE BRIDGE PLAY COMPLETE Edwin B Kantar 20.00
____ GAMESMAN BRIDGE—PLAY BETTER WITH KANTAR Edwin B. Kantar 7.00
____ HOW TO IMPROVE YOUR BRIDGE Alfred Sheinwold 7.00
____ IMPROVING YOUR BIDDING SKILLS Edwin B. Kantar 10.00
____ INTRODUCTION TO DECLARER'S PLAY Edwin B. Kantar 10.00
____ INTRODUCTION TO DEFENDER'S PLAY Edwin B. Kantar 10.00
____ KANTAR FOR THE DEFENSE Edwin B. Kantar 10.00
____ KANTAR FOR THE DEFENSE VOLUME 2 Edwin B. Kantar 10.00
____ TEST YOUR BRIDGE PLAY Edwin B. Kantar 10.00
____ VOLUME 2—TEST YOUR BRIDGE PLAY Edwin B. Kantar 10.00
____ WINNING DECLARER PLAY Dorothy Hayden Truscott 10.00

BUSINESS, STUDY & REFERENCE

____ BRAINSTORMING Charles Clark 10.00
____ CONVERSATION MADE EASY Elliot Russell 5.00
____ EXAM SECRET Dennis B. Jackson 7.00
____ FIX-IT BOOK Arthur Symons 2.00
____ HOW TO DEVELOP A BETTER SPEAKING VOICE M. Hellier 5.00
____ HOW TO SAVE 50% ON GAS & CAR EXPENSES Ken Stansbie 5.00
____ HOW TO SELF-PUBLISH YOUR BOOK & MAKE IT A BEST SELLER Melvin Powers 20.00
____ INCREASE YOUR LEARNING POWER Geoffrey A. Dudley 5.00
____ PRACTICAL GUIDE TO BETTER CONCENTRATION Melvin Powers 5.00
____ PUBLIC SPEAKING MADE EASY Thomas Montalbo 10.00
____ 7 DAYS TO FASTER READING William S. Schaill 7.00
____ SONGWRITER'S RHYMING DICTIONARY Jane Shaw Whitfield 10.00
____ SPELLING MADE EASY Lester D. Basch & Dr. Milton Finkelstein 3.00
____ STUDENT'S GUIDE TO BETTER GRADES J.A. Rickard 3.00
____ YOUR WILL & WHAT TO DO ABOUT IT Attorney Samuel G. King 7.00

CALLIGRAPHY

____ ADVANCED CALLIGRAPHY Katherine Jeffares 7.00
____ CALLIGRAPHY—THE ART OF BEAUTIFUL WRITING Katherine Jeffares 7.00
____ CALLIGRAPHY FOR FUN & PROFIT Anne Leptich & Jacque Evans 10.00
____ CALLIGRAPHY MADE EASY Tina Serafini 7.00

CHESS & CHECKERS

____ BEGINNER'S GUIDE TO WINNING CHESS Fred Reinfeld 10.00
____ CHESS IN TEN EASY LESSONS Larry Evans 10.00
____ CHESS MADE EASY Milton L. Hanauer 5.00
____ CHESS PROBLEMS FOR BEGINNERS Edited by Fred Reinfeld 7.00

___ CHESS TACTICS FOR BEGINNERS Edited by Fred Reinfeld 10.00
___ HOW TO WIN AT CHECKERS Fred Reinfeld 7.00
___ 1001 BRILLIANT WAYS TO CHECKMATE Fred Reinfeld 10.00
___ 1001 WINNING CHESS SACRIFICES & COMBINATIONS Fred Reinfeld 10.00

COOKERY & HERBS

___ CULPEPER'S HERBAL REMEDIES Dr. Nicholas Culpeper 5.00
___ FAST GOURMET COOKBOOK Poppy Cannon 2.50
___ HEALING POWER OF HERBS May Bethel 5.00
___ HEALING POWER OF NATURAL FOODS May Bethel 7.00
___ HERBS FOR HEALTH—HOW TO GROW & USE THEM Louise Evans Doole 7.00
___ HOME GARDEN COOKBOOK—DELICIOUS NATURAL FOOD RECIPES Ken Kraft . 3.00
___ MEATLESS MEAL GUIDE Tomi Ryan & James H. Ryan, M.D. 4.00
___ VEGETABLE GARDENING FOR BEGINNERS Hugh Wilberg 2.00
___ VEGETABLES FOR TODAY'S GARDENS R. Milton Carleton 2.00
___ VEGETARIAN COOKERY Janet Walker 10.00
___ VEGETARIAN COOKING MADE EASY & DELECTABLE Veronica Vezza 3.00

GAMBLING & POKER

___ HOW TO WIN AT POKER Terence Reese & Anthony T. Watkins 10.00
___ SCARNE ON DICE John Scarne 15.00
___ WINNING AT CRAPS Dr. Lloyd T. Commins 10.00
___ WINNING AT GIN Chester Wander & Cy Rice 10.00
___ WINNING AT POKER—AN EXPERT'S GUIDE John Archer 10.00
___ WINNING AT 21—AN EXPERT'S GUIDE John Archer 10.00
___ WINNING POKER SYSTEMS Norman Zadeh 10.00

HEALTH

___ BEE POLLEN Lynda Lyngheim & Jack Scagnetti 5.00
___ COPING WITH ALZHEIMER'S Rose Oliver, Ph.D. & Francis Bock, Ph.D. 10.00
___ HELP YOURSELF TO BETTER SIGHT Margaret Darst Corbett 10.00
___ HOW YOU CAN STOP SMOKING PERMANENTLY Ernest Caldwell 5.00
___ NATURE'S WAY TO NUTRITION & VIBRANT HEALTH Robert J. Scrutton 3.00
___ NEW CARBOHYDRATE DIET COUNTER Patti Lopez-Pereira 2.00
___ REFLEXOLOGY Dr. Maybelle Segal 7.00
___ REFLEXOLOGY FOR GOOD HEALTH Anna Kaye & Don C. Matchan 10.00
___ YOU CAN LEARN TO RELAX Dr. Samuel Gutwirth 5.00

HOBBIES

___ BEACHCOMBING FOR BEGINNERS Norman Hickin 2.00
___ BLACKSTONE'S MODERN CARD TRICKS Harry Blackstone 7.00
___ BLACKSTONE'S SECRETS OF MAGIC Harry Blackstone 7.00
___ COIN COLLECTING FOR BEGINNERS Burton Hobson & Fred Reinfeld 7.00
___ ENTERTAINING WITH ESP Tony 'Doc' Shiels 2.00
___ 400 FASCINATING MAGIC TRICKS YOU CAN DO Howard Thurston 10.00
___ HOW I TURN JUNK INTO FUN AND PROFIT Sari 3.00
___ HOW TO WRITE A HIT SONG AND SELL IT Tommy Boyce 10.00
___ MAGIC FOR ALL AGES Walter Gibson 10.00
___ PLANTING A TREE TreePeople with Andy & Katie Lipkis 13.00
___ STAMP COLLECTING FOR BEGINNERS Burton Hobson 3.00

HORSE PLAYERS' WINNING GUIDES

___ BETTING HORSES TO WIN Les Conklin 10.00
___ ELIMINATE THE LOSERS Bob McKnight 5.00
___ HOW TO PICK WINNING HORSES Bob McKnight 5.00
___ HOW TO WIN AT THE RACES Sam (The Genius) Lewin 5.00
___ HOW YOU CAN BEAT THE RACES Jack Kavanagh 5.00

_____ I WILL Ben Sweetland 10.00
_____ KNIGHT IN RUSTY ARMOR Robert Fisher 5.00
_____ MAGIC IN YOUR MIND U.S. Andersen 15.00
_____ MAGIC OF THINKING SUCCESS Dr. David J. Schwartz 10.00
_____ MAGIC POWER OF YOUR MIND Walter M. Germain 10.00
_____ NEVER UNDERESTIMATE THE SELLING POWER OF A WOMAN Dottie Walters .. 7.00
_____ PRINCESS WHO BELIEVED IN FAIRY TALES Marcia Grad 10.00
_____ PSYCHO-CYBERNETICS Maxwell Maltz, M.D. 10.00
_____ PSYCHOLOGY OF HANDWRITING Nadya Olyanova 10.00
_____ SALES CYBERNETICS Brian Adams 10.00
_____ SECRET OF SECRETS U.S. Andersen 10.00
_____ SECRET POWER OF THE PYRAMIDS U.S. Andersen 7.00
_____ SELF-THERAPY FOR THE STUTTERER Malcolm Frazer 3.00
_____ STOP COMMITTING VOICE SUICIDE Morton Cooper, Ph.D. 10.00
_____ SUCCESS CYBERNETICS U.S. Andersen 10.00
_____ 10 DAYS TO A GREAT NEW LIFE William E. Edwards 3.00
_____ THINK AND GROW RICH Napoleon Hill 10.00
_____ THINK LIKE A WINNER Walter Doyle Staples, Ph.D. 15.00
_____ THREE MAGIC WORDS U.S. Andersen 12.00
_____ TREASURY OF COMFORT Edited by Rabbi Sidney Greenberg 10.00
_____ TREASURY OF THE ART OF LIVING Edited by Rabbi Sidney Greenberg 10.00
_____ WHAT YOUR HANDWRITING REVEALS Albert E. Hughes 4.00
_____ WINNING WITH YOUR VOICE Morton Cooper, Ph.D. 10.00
_____ YOUR SUBCONSCIOUS POWER Charles M. Simmons 7.00

SPORTS
_____ BILLIARDS—POCKET • CAROM • THREE CUSHION Clive Cottingham, Jr. 10.00
_____ COMPLETE GUIDE TO FISHING Vlad Evanoff 2.00
_____ HOW TO IMPROVE YOUR RACQUETBALL Lubarsky, Kaufman & Scagnetti 5.00
_____ HOW TO WIN AT POCKET BILLIARDS Edward D. Knuchell 10.00
_____ JOY OF WALKING Jack Scagnetti 3.00
_____ RACQUETBALL FOR WOMEN Toni Hudson, Jack Scagnetti & Vince Rondone 3.00
_____ SECRET OF BOWLING STRIKES Dawson Taylor 5.00
_____ SOCCER—THE GAME & HOW TO PLAY IT Gary Rosenthal 7.00
_____ STARTING SOCCER Edward F Dolan, Jr. 5.00

TENNIS LOVERS' LIBRARY
_____ HOW TO BEAT BETTER TENNIS PLAYERS Loring Fiske 4.00
_____ PSYCH YOURSELF TO BETTER TENNIS Dr. Walter A. Luszki 2.00
_____ TENNIS FOR BEGINNERS Dr. H.A. Murray 2.00
_____ WEEKEND TENNIS—HOW TO HAVE FUN & WIN AT THE SAME TIME Bill Talbert . 3.00

WILSHIRE PET LIBRARY
_____ DOG TRAINING MADE EASY & FUN John W. Kellogg 5.00
_____ HOW TO BRING UP YOUR PET DOG Kurt Unkelbach 2.00
_____ HOW TO RAISE & TRAIN YOUR PUPPY Jeff Griffen 5.00

Available from your bookstore or directly from Melvin Powers.
Please add $2.00 shipping and handling for each book ordered.

Melvin Powers
12015 Sherman Road
No. Hollywood, California 91605

For our complete catalog, visit our Web site at http://www.mpowers.com.

WILSHIRE HORSE LOVERS' LIBRARY